The Inner
Game
of Tennis

The Inner Game
of Tennis

W. Timothy Gallwey

Random House  New York

Published in the United States by Random House,
Inc., New York, and simultaneously in Canada by Random
House of Canada Limited, Toronto.
Manufactured in the United States of America
First Edition

Library of Congress Cataloging in Publication Data
Gallwey, W. Timothy. The Inner Game of Tennis.
1. Tennis—Psychological aspects. 1. Title.
GV1002.9.P75G34   796.34'2'019   73-20582   ISBN 0-394-49154-8

● for my mother and father
 who brought me to the Game
 and for Guru Maharaj Ji
 who showed me what Winning is

● Men play games because
God first plays a Game.

Contents

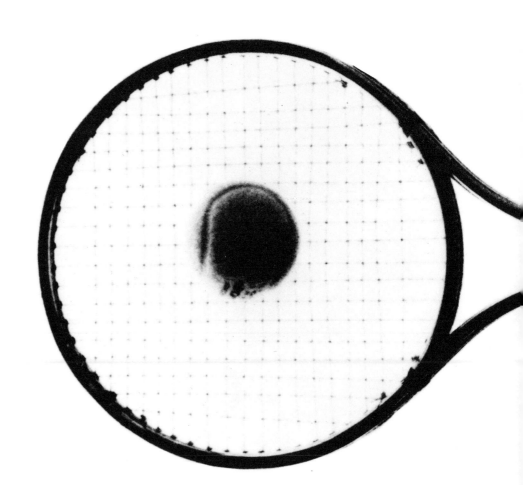

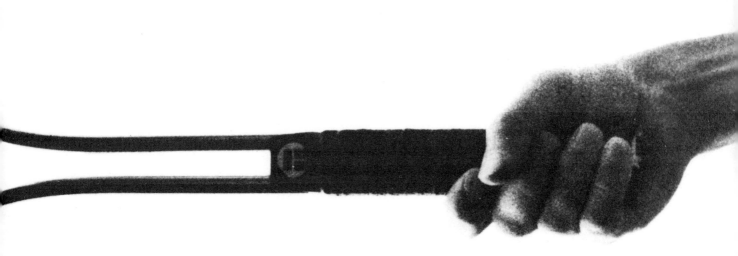

Introduction

Every game is composed of two parts, an outer game and an inner game. The outer game is played against an external opponent to overcome external obstacles, and to reach an external goal. Mastering this game is the subject of many books offering instructions on how to swing a racket, club or bat, and how to position arms, legs or torso to achieve the best results. But for some reason most of us find these instructions easier to remember than to execute.

It is the thesis of this book that neither mastery nor satisfaction can be found in the playing of any game without giving some attention to the relatively neglected skills of the inner game. This is the game that takes place in the mind of the player, and it is played against such obstacles as lapses in concentration, nervousness, self-doubt and self-condemnation. In short, it is played to overcome all habits of mind which inhibit excellence in performance.

We often wonder why we play so well one day and so poorly the next, or why we clutch during competition, or blow easy shots. And why does it take so long to break a bad habit and learn a new one? Victories in the inner game may provide no additions to the trophy case, but they bring valuable rewards which are permanent and which contribute significantly to one's success thereafter, off the court as well as on.

The player of the inner game comes to value the art of relaxed concentration above all other skills; he discovers a true basis for self-confidence; and he learns that the secret to winning any game lies in not trying too hard. He aims at the kind of spontaneous performance which occurs only when the mind is calm and seems at one with the body, which finds its own surprising ways to surpass its own limits again and again. Moreover, while overcoming the common hang-ups of competition, the player of the inner game uncovers a will to win which unlocks all his energy and which is never discouraged by losing.

There is a far more natural and effective process for learning and doing almost anything than most of us realize. It is similar to the process we all used, but soon forgot, as we learned to walk and talk. It uses the so-called unconscious mind more than the deliberate "self-conscious" mind, the spinal and midbrain areas of the nervous system more than the cerebral cortex. This process doesn't have to be learned; we already know it. All that is needed is to *unlearn* those habits which interfere with it and then to just *let it happen*.

To explore the limitless potential within the human body is the quest of the Inner Game; in this book it will be explored through the medium of tennis.

1. Reflections on the Mental Side of Tennis

The problems which most perplex tennis players are not those dealing with the proper way to swing a racket. Books and professionals
giving this information abound. Nor do most players complain
excessively about physical limitations. The most common complaint of sportsmen ringing down the corridors of the ages is,
"It's not that I don't know what to do, it's that I don't do what I
know!" Other common complaints that come constantly to the attention of the tennis pro:

> **When I'm practicing, I play very well, but when I get into a
> match, I fall apart.**
>
> ---
>
> **I know exactly what I'm doing wrong on my forehand, I just can't
> seem to break the habit.**
>
> ---
>
> **When I'm really trying hard to do the stroke the way it says to in
> the book, I flub the shot every time. When I concentrate on one
> thing I'm supposed to be doing, I forget something else.**
>
> ---
>
> **Every time I get near match point against a good player, I get so
> nervous I lose my concentration.**
>
> ---
>
> **I'm my own worst enemy; I usually beat myself.**

Most players of any sport run into these or similar difficulties all
the time, yet there are few professionals and fewer books that deal
with the mental side of sports with any depth of insight. The player
is usually left with such warmed-over aphorisms as, "Well, tennis
is a very psychological game, and you have to develop the proper
mental attitudes. You have to be confident and possess the will to
win or else you'll always be a loser." But how can one "be confident"
or develop the "proper mental attitudes"? These questions are
usually left unanswered.

So there seems to be room for comment on the improvement of
the mental processes which translate the knowledge of how to hit
a ball into the corresponding bodily action. How to develop the
mental skills, without which high performance is impossible, is the
subject of *The Inner Game of Tennis.*

The Typical Tennis Lesson

Imagine what goes on inside the head of an eager student taking a lesson from an equally eager new tennis pro. Suppose that the student is a middle-aged businessman bent on improving his position on the club ladder. The pro is standing at the net with a large basket of balls, and being a bit uncertain whether his student is considering him worth the lesson fee, he is carefully evaluating every shot. "That's good, but you're rolling your racket face over a little on your follow-through, Mr. Weil. Now shift your weight onto your front foot as you step into the ball . . . Now you're taking your racket back too late . . . Your backswing should be a little lower than on that last shot . . . That's it, much better." Before long, Mr. Weil's mind is churning with six thoughts about what he should be doing and sixteen thoughts about what he shouldn't be doing. Improvement seems dubious and very complex, but both he and the pro are impressed by the careful analysis of each stroke and the fee is gladly paid upon receipt of the advice to "practice all this, and eventually you'll see a big improvement."

As a new pro, I too was guilty of overteaching, but one day when I was in a relaxed mood, I began saying less and noticing more. Errors that I saw but didn't mention were correcting themselves without the student ever knowing he had made them. How were the changes happening? Though I found this interesting, it was a little hard on my ego, which didn't quite see how it was going to get its due credit for the improvements being made. It was an even greater blow when I realized that sometimes verbal instruction to a conscientious student seemed to *decrease* the probability of the desired correction occurring.

All teaching pros know what I'm talking about. They all have students like one of mine named Dorothy. I would give Dorothy a gentle, low-pressured instruction like, "Why don't you try lifting the follow-through up from your waist to the level of your shoulder? The topspin will keep the ball in the court." Sure enough, Dorothy would try with everything she had. The muscles would tense around her mouth; her eyebrows would set in a determined frown; the muscles in her forearm would tighten, making fluidity impossible; and the follow-through would end only a few inches higher. At this point, the stock response of the patient pro is, "That's better, Dorothy, but relax, dear, don't try so hard!" The advice is good as far as it goes, but Dorothy does not understand how to "relax."

Why should Dorothy—or you or I—experience an awkward tightening when performing a desired action which is not physically difficult? What happens inside the head between the time the instruction is given and the swing is complete? The first glimmer of an answer to this key question came to me at a moment of rare insight after a lesson with Dorothy: "Whatever's going on in her head, it's too damn much! She's trying too hard, and it's partly my fault." Then and there, I promised myself I would cut down on the quantity of verbal instructions.

My next lesson that day was with a beginner named Paul who had never held a racket. I was determined to show him how to play using as few instructions as possible; I'd try to keep his mind uncluttered and see if it made a difference. So I started by telling Paul I was trying something new: I was going to skip entirely my usual explanations to beginning players about the proper grip, stroke and footwork for the basic forehand. Instead, I was going to hit ten forehands myself, and I wanted him to watch carefully, *not* thinking about what I was doing, but simply trying to grasp a *visual image* of the forehand. He was to repeat the image in his mind several times and then just let his body imitate. After I had hit ten forehands, Paul imagined himself doing the same. Then, as I put the racket into his hand, sliding it into the correct grip, he said to me, "I noticed that the first thing you did was to move your feet." I replied with a noncommittal grunt and asked him to let his body imitate the forehand as well as it could. He dropped the ball, took a perfect backswing, swung forward, racket level, and with natural fluidity ended the swing at shoulder height, perfect for his first attempt! But wait, his feet; they hadn't moved an inch from the perfect ready position he had assumed before taking his racket back. They were nailed to the court. I pointed to them, and Paul said, "Oh yeah, I forgot about them!" The one element of the stroke Paul had tried to remember was the one thing he didn't do! Everything else had been absorbed and reproduced without a word being uttered or an instruction being given!

I was beginning to learn what all good pros and students of tennis must learn: that images are better than words, showing better than telling, too much instruction worse than none, and that conscious trying often produces negative results. One question perplexed me: What's wrong with trying? What does it mean to try *too* hard?

Playing Out of Your Mind

Reflect on the state of mind of a player who is said to be "hot" or "on his game." Is he thinking about how he should hit each shot? Is he thinking at all? Listen to the phrases commonly used to describe a player at his best: "He's out of his mind"; "He's playing over his head"; "He's unconscious"; "He doesn't know what he's doing." The common factor in each of these descriptions is what might be called "mindlessness." There seems to be an intuitive sense that the mind is transcended—or at least in part rendered inoperative. Athletes in most sports use similar phrases, and the best of them know that their peak performance never comes when they're thinking about it.

Clearly, to play unconsciously does not mean to play without consciousness. That would be quite difficult! In fact, someone playing "out of his mind" is more aware of the ball, the court, and, when necessary, his opponent. But he is not aware of giving himself a lot of instructions, thinking about how to hit the ball, how to correct past mistakes or how to repeat what he just did. He is conscious, but not thinking, *not over-trying*. A player in this state knows where he wants the ball to go, but he doesn't have to "try hard" to send it there. It just seems to happen—and often with more accuracy then he could have hoped for. The player seems to be immersed in a flow of action which requires his energy, yet results in greater power and accuracy. The "hot streak" usually continues until he starts thinking about it and tries to maintain it; as soon as he attempts to exercise control, he loses it.

To test this theory is a simple matter, if you don't mind a little underhanded gamesmanship. The next time your opponent is having a hot streak, simply ask him as you switch courts, "Say, George, what are you doing so differently that's making your forehand so good today?" If he takes the bait—and 95 percent will—and begins to think about how he's swinging, telling you how he's really meeting the ball out in front, keeping his wrist firm and following through better, his streak invariably will end. He will lose his timing and fluidity as he tries to repeat what he has just told you he was doing so well.

But can one learn to play "out of his mind" on purpose? How can you be consciously unconscious? It sounds like a contradiction in terms; yet this state can be achieved. Perhaps a better way to describe the player who is "unconscious" is by saying that his mind is so concentrated, so focused, that it is *still*. It becomes one with what the body is doing, and the unconscious or automatic functions are working without interference from thoughts. The concentrated mind has no room for thinking how well the body is doing, much less of the how-to's of the doing. When the player is in this state of concentration, he is really *into* the game; he is at one with racket, ball and stroke; he discovers his true potential.

The ability to approach this state is the goal of the Inner Game. The development of inner skills is required, but it is interesting to note that if, while learning tennis, you begin to learn control of the mind, to concentrate the energy of awareness, you have learned something far more valuable than how to hit a forceful backhand. The backhand can be used to advantage only on a tennis court, but the skill of mastering the art of effortless concentration is invaluable in whatever you set your mind to.

2. The Discovery of the Two Selves

A major breakthrough in my attempts to understand the art of control of mind and body came when, while teaching, I again began to notice what was taking place before my eyes. Listen to the way players talk to themselves on the court: "Come on, Tom, meet the ball in front of you."

We're interested in what is happening inside the player's mind. Who is telling who what? Most players are talking to themselves on the court all the time. "Get up for the ball." "Keep it to his backhand." "Keep your eyes on the ball." "Bend your knees." The commands are endless. For some, it's like hearing a tape recording of the last lesson playing inside their head. Then, after the shot is made, another thought flashes through the mind and might be expressed as follows: "You clumsy ox, your grandmother could play better!" One day I was wondering who was talking to whom. Who was scolding and who being scolded. "I'm talking to myself," say most people. But just who is this "I" and who the "myself"?

Obviously, the "I" and the "myself" are separate entities or there would be no conversation, so one could say that within each player there are two "selves." One, the "I," seems to give instructions; the other, "myself," seems to perform the action. Then "I" returns with an evaluation of the action. For clarity let's call the "teller" Self 1 and the "doer" Self 2.

Now we are ready for the first major postulate of the Inner Game: within each player the kind of relationship that exists between Self 1 and Self 2 is the prime factor in determining one's ability to translate his knowledge of technique into effective action. In other words, the key to better tennis—or better anything—lies in improving the relationship between the conscious teller, Self 1, and the unconscious, automatic doer, Self 2.

The Typical Relationship between Self 1 and Self 2

Imagine that instead of being parts of the same person, Self 1 (teller) and Self 2 (doer) are two separate persons. How would you characterize their relationship after witnessing the following conversation between them? The player on the court is trying to make a stroke improvement. "Okay, dammit, keep your stupid wrist firm," he orders. Then as ball after ball comes over the net, Self 1 reminds Self 2, "Keep it firm. Keep it firm. Keep it firm!" Monotonous? Think how Self 2 must feel! It seems as though Self 1 doesn't think Self 2 hears well, or has a short memory, or is stupid. The truth is, of course, that Self 2, which includes the unconscious mind and nervous system, hears everything, never forgets anything, and is anything but stupid. After hitting the ball firmly once, he knows forever which muscles to contract to do it again. That's his nature.

And what's going on during the hit itself? If you look closely at the face of the player, you will see that his cheek muscles are tightening and his lips are pursed in effort and attempted concentration. But face muscles aren't required to hit the backhand, nor do they help concentration. Who's initiating that effort? Self 1, of course. But why? He's supposed to be the teller, not the doer, but it seems he doesn't really trust 2 to do the job or else he wouldn't have to do all the work himself. This is the nub of the problem: Self 1 does not trust Self 2, even though the unconscious, automatic self is extremely competent.

Back to our player. His muscles tense in over-effort, contact is made with the ball, there is a slight flick of the wrist, and the ball hits the back fence. "You bum, you'll never learn how to hit a backhand," Self 1 complains. By thinking too much and trying too hard, Self 1 has produced tension and muscle conflict in the body. He is responsible for the error, but he heaps the blame on Self 2 and then, by condemning it further, undermines his own confidence in Self 2. As a result the stroke grows worse and frustration builds.

"Trying Hard": A Questionable Virtue

Haven't we been told since childhood that we're never going to amount to anything unless we try hard? So what does it mean when we observe someone who is trying too hard? Is it best to try medium hard? Or might the answer depend on the person doing the trying? Equipped with the concept of the two selves, see if you can answer this seeming paradox for yourself after reading the following illustration. Watch the Zen paradox of "effortless effort" dissolve.

One day while I was wondering about these matters, a very cheery and attractive housewife came to me for a lesson complaining that she was about to give up the game of tennis. She was really very discouraged because, as she said, "I'm really not well coordinated at all. I want to get good enough that my husband will ask me to play mixed doubles with him without making it sound like a family obligation." When I asked her what the problem seemed to be, she said, "For one thing, I can't hit the ball on the strings; most of the time I hit it on the wood."

"Let's take a look," I said, reaching into my basket of balls. I hit her ten waist-high forehands near enough so that she didn't have to move for them. I was surprised that she hit eight out of ten balls either directly on the wood or partly on the strings, partly on the frame. Yet her stroke was good enough. I was puzzled. She hadn't been exaggerating her problem. I wondered if it was her eyesight, but she assured me that her eyes were perfect.

So I told Joan we'd try a few experiments. First I asked her to try very hard to hit the ball on the center of the racket. I was guessing that this might produce even worse results, which would prove my point about trying too hard. But new theories don't always pan out; besides, it takes a lot of talent to hit eight out of ten balls on the narrow frame of a racket. This time, she managed to hit only six balls on the wood. Next, I told her to try to hit the balls on the frame. This time she hit only four on the wood and made good contact with six. She was a bit surprised, but took the chance to give her Self 2 a knock, saying, "Oh, I can never do anything I try to!" Actually, she was close to an important truth. It was becoming clear that her way of trying wasn't helpful.

So before hitting the next set of balls, I asked Joan, "This time I want you to focus your mind on the seams of the ball. Don't think about making contact. In fact, don't try to hit the ball at all. Just *let* your racket contact the ball where *it* wants to, and we'll see what happens." Joan looked more relaxed, and her racket proceeded to hit nine out of ten balls dead center! Only the last ball caught the frame. I asked her if she was aware of what was going through her mind as she swung at the last ball. "Sure," she replied with a lilt in her voice, "I was thinking I might make a tennis player after all." She was right.

Joan was beginning to sense the difference between "trying hard," the energy of Self 1, and "effort," the energy used by Self 2, to do the work necessary. During the last set of balls, Self 1 was fully occupied in watching the seams of the ball. As a result, Self 2 was able to do its own thing unimpaired, and it proved to be pretty good at it. Even Self 1 was starting to recognize the talents of 2; she was getting them together.

Getting it together mentally in tennis involves the learning of several internal skills: 1) learning to program your computer Self 2 with images rather than instructing yourself with words; 2) learning to "trust thyself" (Self 2) to do what you (Self 1) ask of it. This means letting Self 2 hit the ball and 3) learning to see "nonjudgmentally" —that is, to see what is happening rather than merely noticing how well or how badly it is happening. This overcomes "trying too hard." All these skills are subsidiary to the master skill, without which nothing of value is ever achieved: the art of concentration.

The Inner Game of Tennis will next explore a way to learn these skills, using tennis as a medium.

3. Getting It Together

Part One: Quieting the Mind

We have arrived at a key point: it is the constant "thinking" activity of Self 1, the ego-mind, which causes interference with the natural *doing* processes of Self 2. Harmony between the two selves exists when the mind itself is quiet. Only when the mind is still is one's peak performance reached.

When a tennis player is "on his game," he's not thinking about how, when, or even where to hit the ball. He's not *trying* to hit the ball, and after the shot he doesn't think about how badly or how well he made contact. The ball seems to get hit through an automatic process which doesn't require thought. There may be an awareness of the sight, sound and feel of the ball, and even of the tactical situation, but the player just seems to *know* without thinking what to do.

Listen to how D. T. Suzuki, the renowned Zen master, describes the effects of the ego-mind on archery in his foreword to *Zen in the Art of Archery:*

> **As soon as we reflect, deliberate, and conceptualize, the original unconsciousness is lost and a thought interferes . . . The arrow is off the string but does not fly straight to the target, nor does the target stand where it is. Calculation, which is miscalculation, sets in . . .**
>
> ---
>
> **Man is a thinking reed but his great works are done when he is not calculating and thinking. "Childlikeness" has to be restored with long years of training in self-forgetfulness.**

Perhaps this is why it is said that great poetry is born in silence. Great music and art are said to arise from the quiet depths of the unconscious, and true expressions of love are said to come from a source which lies beneath words and thoughts. So it is with the greatest efforts in sports; they come when the mind is as still as a glass lake.

Such moments have been called "peak experiences" by the humanistic psychologist Dr. Abraham Maslow. Researching the common characteristics of persons having such experiences, he reports the following descriptive phrases: "He feels more integrated" [the two selves are one], "feels at one with the experience," "is relatively egoless" [quiet mind], "feels at the peak of his powers," "fully functioning," "is in the groove," "effortless," "free of blocks, inhibitions, cautions, fears, doubts, controls, reservations, self-criticisms, brakes," "he is spontaneous and more creative," "is most here-now," "is non-striving, non-needing, non-wishing . . . he just is."

If you reflect upon your own highest moments or peak experiences, it is likely that you will recall feelings that these phrases describe. You will probably also remember them as moments of great pleasure, even ecstasy. During such experiences, the mind does not act like a separate entity telling you what you should do or criticizing how you do it. It is quiet; you are "together," and the action flows as free as a river.

When this happens on the tennis court, we are concentrating without *trying* to concentrate. We feel spontaneous and alert. We have an inner assurance that we can do what needs to be done, without having to "try hard." We simply *know* the action will come, and when it does, we don't feel like taking credit; rather, we feel fortunate, "graced." As Suzuki says, we become "childlike."

The image comes to my mind of the balanced movement of a cat stalking a bird. Effortlessly alert, he crouches, gathering his relaxed muscles for the spring. No thinking about when to jump, nor how he will push off with his hind legs to attain the proper distance, his mind is still and perfectly concentrated on his prey. No thought flashes into his consciousness of the possibility or consequences of missing his mark. He sees only bird. Suddenly the bird takes off; at the same instant, the cat leaps. With perfect anticipation he intercepts his dinner two feet off the ground. Perfectly, thoughtlessly executed action, and afterward, no self-congratulations, just the reward inherent in his action: the bird in the mouth.

In rare moments, tennis players approach the unthinking spontaneity of the leopard. These moments seem to occur most frequently when players are volleying back and forth at the net. Often the exchange of shots at such short quarters is so rapid that action faster than thought is required. These moments are exhilarating, and the players are often amazed to find that they make perfect placements against shots they didn't even expect to reach. Moving more quickly than they thought they could, they have no time to plan; the perfect shot just comes. And feeling that they didn't execute the shot deliberately, they often call it luck; but if it happens repeatedly, one begins to trust oneself and feel a deep sense of confidence.

In short, "getting it together" requires slowing the mind. Quieting the mind means less thinking, calculating, judging, worrying, fearing, hoping, trying, regretting, controlling, jittering or distracting. The mind is still when it is totally here and now in perfect oneness with the action and the actor. It is the purpose of the Inner Game to increase the frequency and the duration of these moments, quieting the mind by degrees and realizing thereby a continual expansion of our capacity to learn and perform.

At this point the question naturally arises: "How can I still my mind?" Or "How can I keep from thinking on the tennis court?" The answer is simple: just stop! As an experiment the reader might want to put down this book for a minute and simply stop thinking. See how long you can remain in a perfectly thoughtless state. One minute? Ten seconds? If you were able to quiet your mind, there is no reason to read further in this book because you already know the key to a concentrated mind, and thereby the secret that reveals all life's other secrets and the source of truth and joy. More than likely, however, you found it difficult, perhaps impossible, to still the mind completely. One thought led to another, then to another, etc.

For most of us, quieting the mind is a gradual process involving the learning of several inner skills. These inner skills are really arts of forgetting mental habits acquired since we were children.

The first skill to learn is the art of letting go the human inclination to judge ourselves and our performance as either good or bad. Letting go of the judging process is a basic key to the Inner Game; its meaning will emerge as you read the remainder of this chapter. When we *un*learn how to be judgmental, it is possible to achieve spontaneous, concentrated play.

Letting Go of Judgments

To see the process of judgment in action, observe almost any tennis match or lesson. Watch closely the face of the hitter and you will see expressions of judgmental thoughts occurring in his mind. Frowns occur after each "bad" shot, and expressions of self-satisfaction after every shot judged as particularly "good." Often the judgments will be expressed verbally in a vocabulary which ranges widely, depending on the player and the degree of his like or dislike of his shot. Sometimes the judgment is most clearly perceived in the tone of voice used rather than the words themselves. The declaration, "You rolled your racket over again," can be said as a biting self-criticism or a simple observation of fact, depending on the tone of voice. The imperatives, "Watch the ball," or "Move your feet," can be uttered as an encouragement to the body or as a belittling condemnation of its past performance.

To understand more clearly what is meant by judgment, imagine a singles match being played by Mr. A and Mr. B, with Mr. C acting as the umpire. Mr. A is serving his second serve to Mr. B on the first point of a tie-breaker. The ball lands wide, and Mr. C calls, "Out. Double fault." Seeing his serve land out and hearing, "Double fault," Mr. A frowns, says something demeaning about himself, and calls the serve "terrible." Seeing the same stroke, Mr. B. judges it as "good" and smiles. The umpire neither frowns nor smiles; he simply calls the ball as he sees it.

What is important to see here is that neither the "goodness" nor "badness" ascribed to the event by the players is an attribute of the shot itself. Rather, they are evaluations *added* to the event in the minds of the players according to their individual reactions. Mr. A is saying, in effect, "I don't like that event"; Mr. B is saying, "I like that event." The umpire, here ironically called the judge, doesn't judge the event as positive or negative; he simply sees the ball land and calls it out. If the event occurs several more times, Mr. A will get very upset, Mr. B will continue to be pleased, and the umpire, sitting above the scene, will still be noting with detached interest all that is happening.

What I mean by judgment is the act of assigning a negative or positive value to an event. In effect it is saying that some events within your experience are good and you like them, and other events in your experience are bad and you don't like them. You don't like the sight of yourself hitting a ball into the net, but you judge as good the sight of your opponent being aced by your serve. Thus, judgments are our personal, ego reactions to the sights, sounds, feelings and thoughts within our experience.

What does this have to do with tennis? Well, it is the initial act of judgment which provokes a thinking process. First the player's mind judges one of his shots as bad or good. If he judges it as bad, he begins thinking about what was wrong with it. Then he tells himself how to correct it. Then he *tries* hard, giving himself instructions as he does so. Finally he evaluates again. Obviously the mind is anything but still and the body is tight with trying. If the shot is evaluated as good, Self 1 starts wondering how he hit such a good shot; then tries to get his body to repeat the process by giving self-instructions, trying hard, and so on. Both mental processes end in further evaluation, which perpetuates the process of thinking and self-conscious performance. As a consequence, the player's muscles tighten when they need to be loose, strokes become awkward and less fluid, and negative evaluations are likely to continue with growing intensity.

After Self 1 has evaluated several shots, he is likely to start generalizing. Instead of judging a single event as "another bad backhand," he starts thinking, "You have a terrible backhand." Instead of saying, "You were nervous on that point," he generalizes, "You're the worst choke artist in the club." Other common judgmental generalizations are, "I'm having a bad day," "I always miss the easy ones," "I'm slow," etc.

It is interesting to see how the judgmental mind extends itself. It may begin by complaining, "What a lousy serve," then extend to "I'm serving badly today." After a few more "bad" serves, the judgment may become further extended to "I have a terrible serve." Then, "I'm a lousy tennis player," and finally, "I'm no good." First the mind judges the event, then groups events, then identifies with the combined event, and finally judges itself.

As a result, what usually happens is that these self-judgments become self-fulfilling prophecies. That is, they are communications from Self 1 about Self 2 which, after being repeated often enough, are believed by Self 2. Then Self 2, acting like the computer he is, begins to live up to these expectations. If you tell yourself often enough that you are a poor server, a kind of hypnotic process takes place. It's as if Self 2 is being given a role to play—the role of bad server—and he plays it to the hilt, suppressing for the time being his true capabilities. Once the judgmental mind establishes a self-identity based on its negative judgments, the role-playing continues to hide the true potential of Self 2 until the hypnotic spell is broken. Most players would do well to heed the wisdom of ancient yoga philosophy: "You become what you think."

After a number of bad backhands are hit, and the player tells himself that he has a bad backhand, or at least that his backhand is "off," he often goes to a pro to get it repaired. It is my experience that players come to tennis pros in the same frame of mind that patients go to doctors: as if they are sick and want to be cured. This kind of judgment is so pervasive in our culture that it is taken for granted. It would seem strange to take a tennis lesson when you didn't see anything wrong with your game. Any pro knows, however, that it is easier to help a player who is on his game improve than it is to help one who considers he is playing poorly. (In China, people make regular visits to doctors when they are healthy. The doctor's job is more to keep people healthy than it is to cure them of sickness. If a Chinese follows his doctor's instructions and *then* gets sick, he is likely to change doctors.) Why not go to a tennis pro accepting your game as it is?

When asked to give up making judgments about one's game, the judgmental mind usually protests, "But if I can't hit a backhand inside the court to save my life, do you expect me to ignore my faults and pretend my game is fine?" Be clear about this: letting go of judgments does not mean ignoring errors. It simply means seeing events as they are and not adding anything to them. Nonjudgmental awareness might observe that during a certain match you hit 50 percent of your first serves into the net. It doesn't ignore the fact. It may accurately describe your serve on that day as erratic and seek to discover the causes. Judgment begins when the serve is labeled "bad" and causes interference with one's playing when a reaction of anger, frustration or discouragement follows. If the judgment process could be stopped with the naming of the event as bad, and there were no further ego reactions, then the interference would be minimal. But judgmental labels usually lead to emotional reactions and then to tightness, trying too hard, self-condemnation, etc. This process can be slowed by using descriptive but nonjudgmental words to describe the events you see.

If a judgmental player comes to me, I will do my best not to believe his tale of a *bad* backhand or of the *bad* player who has it. If he hits the balls out, I will notice they go out, and I may notice the reason why they are going out. But is there a need to judge him or the backhand as sick? If I do, I am likely to get as uptight in the process of correcting him as he is likely to be in correcting himself. Judgment results in tightness, and tightness interferes with the fluidity required for accurate and quick movement. Relaxation produces smooth strokes and results from accepting your strokes as they are, even if erratic.

Read this simple analogy and see if an alternative to the judging process doesn't begin to emerge. When we plant a rose seed in the earth, we notice that it is small, but we do not criticize it as "rootless and stemless." We treat it as a seed, giving it the water and nourishment required of a seed. When it first shoots up out of the earth, we don't condemn it as immature and underdeveloped; nor do we criticize the buds for not being open when they appear. We stand in wonder at the process taking place and give the plant the care it needs at each stage of its development. The rose is a rose from the time it is a seed to the time it dies. Within it, at all times, it contains its whole potential. It seems to be constantly in the process of change; yet at each state, at each moment, it is perfectly all right as it is.

Similarly, the errors we make can be seen as an important part of the developing process. In its process of developing, our tennis game learns a great deal from errors. Even slumps are part of the process. They are not *bad* events, but they seem to endure endlessly as long as we call them bad and identify with them. Like a good gardener who knows when the soil needs alkaline and when acid, the competent tennis pro should be able to help the development of your game. Usually the first thing that needs to be done is to deal with the negative concepts inhibiting the innate developmental process. Both the pro and the player stimulate this process as they begin to see and to accept the strokes as they are at that moment.

The first step is to see your strokes as they are. They must be perceived clearly. This can be done only when personal judgment is absent. As soon as a stroke is seen clearly and accepted as it is, a natural and speedy process of change begins.

The example below, a true story, illustrates the key to unblocking the natural development in our strokes.

Discovering the Process

One day when I was teaching a group of men at John Gardiner's Tennis Ranch in Carmel Valley, California, a businessman realized how much more power and control he got on his backhand when his racket was taken back below the level of the ball. He was so enthusiastic about his "new" stroke that he rushed to tell his friend Jack about it as if some kind of miracle had occurred. Jack, who considered his erratic backhand one of the major problems of his life, came rushing up to me during the lunch hour, exclaiming, "I've always had a terrible backhand. Maybe you can help me."

I asked, "What's so terrible about your backhand?"

"I take my racket back too high on my backswing."

"How do you know?"

"Because at least five different pros have told me so. I just haven't been able to correct it."

For a brief moment I was aware of the absurdity of the situation. Here was a business executive who controlled large commercial enterprises of great complexity asking me for help as if he had no control over his own right arm. Why wouldn't it be possible, I wondered, to give him the simple reply, "Sure, I can help you. L-o-w-e-r y-o-u-r r-a-c-k-e-t!"

But complaints such as Jack's are common among people of all levels of intelligence and proficiency. Besides, it was clear that at least five other pros had told him to lower his racket without much effect. What was keeping him from doing it I wondered.

I asked Jack to take a few swings on the patio where we were standing. His backswing started back very low, but then, sure enough, just before swinging forward it lifted to the level of his shoulder and swung down into the imagined ball. The five pros were right. I asked him to swing several more times without making any comment. "Isn't that better?" he asked. "I tried to keep it low." But each time just before swinging forward, his racket lifted; it was obvious that had he been hitting an actual ball, the underspin imparted by the downward swing would have caused it to sail out.

"Your backhand is all right," I said reassuringly. "It's just going through some changes. Why don't you take a closer look at it." We walked over to a large windowpane and there I asked him to swing again while watching his reflection. He did so, again taking his characteristic hitch at the back of his swing, but this time he was astounded. "Hey, I really do take my racket back high! It goes up above my shoulder!" There was no judgment in his voice; he was just reporting with amazement what his eyes had seen.

What surprised me was Jack's surprise. Hadn't he said that five pros had told him his racket was too high? I was certain that if I had told him the same thing after his first swing, he would have replied, "Yes, I know." But what was now clear was that he didn't *really* know, since no one is ever surprised at seeing something they already know. Despite all those lessons, he had never *directly* experienced his racket going back high. His mind had been so absorbed in the process of judgment and trying to change this "bad" stroke that he had never perceived the stroke itself.

Looking in the glass which mirrored his stroke as it was, Jack was able to keep his racket low quite effortlessly as he swung again. "That feels entirely different than any backhand I've ever swung," he declared. By now he was swinging up through the ball over and over again. Interestingly, he wasn't congratulating himself for doing it right; he was simply absorbed in how different it *felt*.

After lunch I threw Jack a few balls and he was able to remember how the stroke felt and to repeat the action. This time he just felt where his racket was going, letting his sense of feel replace the visual image offered by the mirror. It was a new experience for him. Soon he was consistently hitting topspin backhands into the court with an effortlessness that made it appear this was his natural swing. In ten minutes he was feeling "in the groove," and he paused to express his gratitude. "I can't tell you how much I appreciate what you've done for me. I've learned more in ten minutes from you than in twenty hours of lessons I've taken on my backhand." I could feel something inside me begin to puff up as it absorbed these "good" words. At the same time, I didn't know quite how to handle this lavish compliment, and found myself hemming and hawing, trying to come up with an appropriately modest reply. Then, for a moment, my mind turned off and I realized that I hadn't given Jack a single instruction on his backhand! I thanked him for his praise, and then asked, "But what did I teach you?" He was quiet for a full half-minute, trying to remember what I had told him. Finally he said, "I can't remember your telling me anything! You were just watching me, but I sure learned a lot." He had learned without being taught.

I can't describe how good I felt at that moment, or why. Tears even began to come to my eyes. I had learned and he had learned, but there was no one there to take credit. There was only the glimmer of a realization that we were both participating in a wonderful process.

The key that unlocked Jack's new backhand—which was really there all the time just waiting to be let out—was that in the instant he stopped trying to change his backhand, he saw it as it was. At first, with the aid of the mirror, he directly *experienced* his backswing. Without thinking or analyzing, he increased his awareness of that part of his swing. When the mind is free of any thought or judgment, it is still and acts like a perfect mirror. Then and only then can we know things as they are.

Seeing, Feeling, and Awareness of What Is

In the game of tennis there are two important things to know. The first is where the ball is. The second is where the racket head is. From the time anyone begins to learn tennis, he is told the importance of watching the ball. It's very simple: you come to know where the ball is by looking at it. You don't have to think, "Oh, here comes the ball; it's clearing the net by about one foot and coming pretty fast. It should bounce near the base line, and I'd better hit it on the rise." No, you simply watch the ball and let the proper response take place.

In the same way, you don't have to think about where your racket head *should* be, but you should realize the importance of being aware of where the racket head *is* at all times. You can't look at it to know where it is because you're watching the ball. You must *feel* it. Feeling it gives you the knowledge of where it is. Knowing where it *should be* isn't feeling where it is. Knowing what your racket *didn't do* isn't feeling where it is. *Feeling* where it is is *knowing* where it is.

No matter what a person's complaint when he has a lesson with me, I have found that the most beneficial first step is to encourage him to *see* and *feel* what he is doing—that is, to increase his awareness of *what actually is.* I follow the same process when my own strokes get out of their groove. But to see things as they are, we must take off our judgmental glasses, whether they're dark or rose-tinted. This action unlocks a process of natural development which is as surprising as it is beautiful.

For example, suppose that a player complains that the timing on his forehand is off. I wouldn't give him an analysis of what is wrong and then instruct him, "Take your racket back sooner," or "Hit the ball farther out in front of you." Instead I might simply ask him to put his attention on where his racket head is at the moment the ball bounces on his side of the net. Since this is not a common instruction, it is likely that the player will never have been told anything about where his racket should or shouldn't be at that particular moment. If his judgmental mind is engaged, he is likely to become a little nervous, since Self 1 likes to try to do things "right" and is nervous when he doesn't know the rightness or wrongness of a particular action. So at once the player may ask where his racket should be when the ball is bouncing. But I decline to say, asking him only to observe where his racket *is* at that moment.

After he hits a few balls, I ask him to tell me where his racket was at the moment in question. The typical reply is, "I'm taking my racket back too late. I know what I'm doing wrong, but I can't stop it." This is a common response of players of all sports, and is the cause of a great deal of frustration.

"Forget about right and wrong for now," I suggest. "Just observe your racket at the moment of bounce." After five or ten more balls are hit to him, the player is likely to reply, "I'm doing better; I'm getting it back earlier."

"Yes, and where was your racket?" I ask.

"I don't know, but I think I was getting it back on time . . . wasn't I?"

Uncomfortable without a standard for right and wrong, the judgmental mind makes up standards of its own. Meanwhile, attention is taken off what *is* and placed on the process of trying to do things right. Even though he may be getting his racket back earlier and is hitting the ball more solidly, he is still in the dark about where his racket is. (If the player is left in this state, thinking that he has found the "secret" to his problem—that is, getting his racket back earlier—he will be momentarily pleased. He will go out eagerly to play and repeat to himself before hitting every forehand, "Get it back early, get it back early, get it back early . . ." For a while this magic phrase will seem to produce "good" results. But after a while, he will start missing again in spite of his self-reminder, will wonder what's going "wrong" and will come back to the pro for another tip.)

So instead of stopping the process at the point where the player is judging positively, I again ask him to observe his racket and to tell me exactly where it is at the moment of bounce. As the player finally lets himself observe his racket with detachment and interest, he can feel what it is actually doing and his awareness increases. Then, without any effort to correct, he will discover that his swing has begun to develop a natural rhythm. In fact, he will find the perfect rhythm for himself, which may be slightly different from what might be dictated by some universal standard called "correct." Then when he goes out to play, he has no magic phrase that must be repeated, and can concentrate without thinking.

What I have tried to illustrate is that there is a natural learning process which operates within everyone—if it is allowed to. This process is waiting to be discovered by all those who do not know of its existence. There is no need to take my word for it; it can be discovered for yourself if it hasn't been already. If it has been experienced, trust it. (This is the subject of Chapter 4.) To discover this natural learning process, it is necessary to let go of the old process of *correcting* faults; that is, it is necessary to let go of judgment and see what happens. Will your strokes develop under the effect of noncritical attention or won't they? Test this.

What about Positive Thinking?

Before finishing with the subject of the judgmental mind, something needs to be said about "positive thinking." The "bad" effects of negative thinking are frequently discussed these days. Books and articles advise readers to replace negative thinking with positive thinking. People are advised to stop telling themselves they are ugly, uncoordinated, unhappy, or whatever, and to repeat to themselves that they are attractive, well coordinated and happy. The substituting of a kind of "positive hypnotism" for a previous habit of "negative hypnotism" may appear at least to have short-range benefits, but I have always found that the honeymoon ends all too soon.

One of the first lessons I learned as a teaching pro was not to find fault with any pupil or even his strokes. So I stopped criticizing either. Instead, I would compliment the pupil when I could, and make only positive suggestions about how to correct his strokes. Some time later, I found myself no longer complimenting my students. The realization that preceded this change occurred one day when I was giving a group of women a lesson on footwork.

I had made a few introductory remarks about self-criticism when Clare, one of the women, asked, "I can understand that negative thinking is harmful, but what about complimenting yourself when you do well? What about positive thinking?" My answer to her was vague — "Well, I don't think positive thinking is as harmful as negative thinking" — but during the lesson that followed, I came to see the issue more clearly.

At the beginning of the lesson, I told the women that I was going to hit each of them six running forehands, and that I wanted them simply to become aware of their feet. "Get in touch with how your feet move getting into position, and whether there is any transfer of weight as you hit the ball." I told them that there was no right and wrong to think about; they were only to observe their own footwork with full attention. While I hit the balls to them, I made no comments. I watched intently what was happening before my eyes, but expressed no judgment either positive or negative. Similarly, the women were quiet, watching each other without comment. They each seemed absorbed in the simple process of experiencing the movement of their feet.

After the series of thirty balls, I noticed that there were no balls at the net; they were all bunched together in the crosscourt area on my side. "Look," I said, "all the balls are together in the corner, and not one at the net." Although semantically this remark was simply an observation of fact, my tone of voice revealed that I was pleased with what I saw. I was complimenting them, and indirectly I was complimenting myself as their instructor.

To my surprise, the girl who was due to hit next said, "Oh, you would have to say that just before my turn!" Though she was half kidding, I could see that she was a little nervous. I repeated the same instructions as before and hit thirty more balls without comment. This time there were frowns appearing on the women's faces and their footwork seemed a little more awkward than before. After the thirtieth ball, there were eight balls at the net and the balls behind me were quite scattered.

Inwardly I criticized myself for having spoiled the magic. Then Clare, the girl who had originally asked me about positive thinking, exclaimed, "Oh, I ruined it for everyone. I was the first to hit a ball into the net, and I hit four of them." I was amazed, as were the others, because it wasn't true. It was another person who had netted the first ball, and Clare had hit only two balls into the net. Her judgmental mind had distorted her perception of what had actually happened.

Then I asked the women if they were aware of something different going through their minds during the second series of balls. Each of them reported being less aware of their feet and more intent on trying to keep from hitting balls into the net. They were trying to live up to an expectation, a standard of right and wrong, which they felt had been set before them. This was exactly what had been missing during the first set of balls. I began to see that my compliment had engaged their judgmental minds. Self 1, the ego-mind, had gotten into the act.

Through this experience, I began to see how Self 1 operated. Always looking for approval and wanting to avoid disapproval, this subtle ego-mind sees a compliment as a potential criticism. He reasons, "If the pro is pleased with one kind of performance, he will be displeased by the opposite. If he likes me for doing well, he will dislike me for not doing well." The standard of good and bad had been established, and the inevitable result was divided concentration and ego-interference.

The women also began to realize the cause of their tightness on the third round of balls. Then Clare seemed to light up like a 1000-watt bulb. "Oh, I see!" she exclaimed, slapping her hand to her forehead. "Compliments are criticisms in disguise! Both are used to manipulate behavior, and compliments are just more socially acceptable!" Whereupon she ran off the court saying she had to find her husband. Evidently she had seen the connection between what she had learned on the tennis court and some other aspect of her life which was important to her, for an hour later I saw her with her husband, still absorbed in intense conversation.

Clearly, positive and negative evaluations are relative to each other. It is impossible to judge one event as positive without seeing other events as not positive or as negative. There is no way to stop just the negative side of the judgmental process. To see your strokes as they are, there is no need to attribute goodness or badness to them. The same goes for the results of your strokes. You can notice exactly how far out a ball lands without labeling it a "bad" event. By ending judgment, you do not avoid seeing what is. Ending judgment means you neither add nor subtract from the facts before your eyes. Things appear as they are—undistorted. In this way, the mind becomes more calm.

"But," protests Self 1, "if I see my ball going out and I don't evaluate it as bad, I won't have any incentive to change it. If I don't dislike what I'm doing wrong, how am I going to change it?" Self 1, the ego-mind, wants to take responsibility for making things "better." He wants the credit for playing an important role in things. He also worries and suffers a lot when things don't go his way.

The following chapter will deal with an alternative process: a process by which actions flow spontaneously and sensibly without an ego-mind on the scene chasing positives and trying to reform negatives. But before concluding this chapter, read this profound but deceptively simple story told me by a much respected friend of mine named Bill.

Three men in a car are driving down a city street early one morning. For the sake of analogy, suppose that each man represents a different kind of tennis player. The man sitting on the right is a positive thinker who believes that his game is great and is full of self-esteem because his tennis is so superior. He's also a self-admitted playboy who enjoys all the good things of life. The man sitting in the middle is a negative thinker who is constantly analyzing what is wrong with himself and his game. He is always involved in some kind of self-improvement program. The third man, who is driving, is in the process of letting go of value judgments altogether. He plays the Inner Game, enjoying things as they are and doing what seems sensible at the moment.

The car pulls up at a stoplight, and crossing the street in front of the car is a beautiful young lady who catches the attention of all three men. Her beauty is particularly apparent because she is wearing no clothes.

The man on the right becomes engrossed in thoughts of how nice it would be to be with this lady under other circumstances. His mind races through past memories and future fantasies of sensual pleasures. As he reminds himself what a great lover he is, he breathes heavily, causing fog to form on the windshield and slightly dimming the view for the others.

The man sitting in the middle is seeing an example of modern decadence. He's not sure that he should be looking closely at the girl. First miniskirts, he thinks, then topless dancers, then bottomless dancers, and now they're out on the streets in broad daylight! Something must be done to stop all this! He thinks that he should begin by straightening out the playboy on his right.

The driver is seeing the same girl that the others are observing, but is simply watching what is before his eyes. Since his ego is uninvolved, he sees neither good nor bad, and as a result, a detail comes to his attention which was not noticed by either of his companions: the girl's eyes are shut. He realizes that the lady is sleepwalking, and his response is immediate and uncalculating. He stops the car, steps out and puts his coat over the woman's shoulders. He gently wakes her and explains to her that she must have been sleepwalking and offers to take her home.

My friend Bill used to end the story with a twinkle in his eye, saying, "There he received the rewards of his action," leaving each listener to hear what he would.

The first inner skill to be developed in the Inner Game is that of nonjudgmental awareness. When we "unlearn" judgment we discover, usually with some surprise, that we don't need the motivation of a reformer to change our "bad" habits. There is a more natural process of learning and performing waiting to be discovered. It is waiting to show what it can do when allowed to operate without interference from the conscious strivings of the judgmental ego-mind. The discovery of and reliance upon this process is the subject of the next chapter.

4. Getting It Together

Part Two: Letting It Happen

The thesis of the last chapter was that the first step in bringing a greater harmony between ego-mind and body—that is, between Self 1 and Self 2—was to let go of self-judgment. Only when Self 1 stops sitting in judgment over Self 2 and its actions can he become aware of who and what Self 2 is and appreciate the processes by which he works. As this step occurs, trust is developed, and eventually the basic but elusive ingredient for all top performance emerges—self-confidence.

Who and What is Self 2?

Put aside for a moment the opinions you have about your body— whether you think of it as clumsy, uncoordinated, average, or really fantastic—and think about what it does. As you read these very words your body is performing a remarkable piece of coordination. Eyes are moving effortlessly, taking in images of black and white which are automatically compared with memories of similar markings, translated into symbols, then connected with other symbols to form an impression of meaning. Thousands of these operations are taking place every few seconds. At the same time, again without conscious effort, your heart is pumping and your breath is going in and out, keeping a fantastically complicated system of organs, glands and muscles nourished and working. Without conscious effort, billions of cells are functioning, reproducing and fighting off disease.

If you walked to a chair and turned on a light before beginning to read, your body coordinated a great number of muscle movements to accomplish those tasks without help from the conscious mind. Self 1 did not have to tell your body how far to reach before closing your fingers on the light switch; you knew your goal, and your body did what was necessary without thought. The process by which the body learned and performed these actions is no different from the process by which it learns and plays the game of tennis.

Reflect on the complicated series of actions performed by Self 2 in the process of returning a serve. In order to anticipate how and where to move the feet and whether to take the racket back on the forehand or backhand side, the brain must calculate within a fraction of a second the moment the ball leaves the server's racket approximately where it is going to land and where the racket will intercept it. Into this calculation must be computed the initial velocity of the ball, combined with an input for the progressive decrease in velocity and the effect of wind and of spin, to say nothing of the complicated trajectories involved. Then, each of these factors must be recalculated after the bounce of the ball to anticipate the point where contact will be made by the racket. Simultaneously, muscle orders must be given—not just once, but constantly refined on updated information. Finally, the muscles have to respond in cooperation with one another: a movement of feet occurs, the racket is taken back at a certain speed and height, and the face of the racket is kept at a constant angle as the racket and body move forward in balance. Contact is made at a precise point according to whether the order was given to hit down the line or cross-court—an order not given until after a split-second analysis of the movement and balance of the opponent on the other side of the net.

If Pancho Gonzalez is serving, you have approximately .613 seconds to accomplish all this, but even if you are returning the serve of an average player, you will have only about 1 second. Just to hit the ball is clearly a remarkable feat; to return it with consistency and accuracy is a mind-boggling achievement. Yet it is not uncommon. The truth is that everyone who inhabits a human body possesses a remarkable creation.

In the light of this, it seems inappropriate to call our bodies derogatory names. Self 2—that is, the physical body, including the brain, memory bank (conscious and unconscious), and the nervous system—is a tremendously sophisticated and competent servant. Inherent within it is an inner intelligence which is staggering. What it doesn't already know, this inner intelligence learns with childlike ease. It uses billions of memory cells and neurological communication circuits. If modern man undertook to create an electronic memory of a capacity equal to the human one by using the most sophisticated computer parts yet devised, the finished product would be, according to a friend of mine who is a computer expert, larger than three Empire State Buildings. Furthermore, no computer yet made is capable of doing the calculations and giving the necessary muscle orders involved in returning a fast serve in the time required.

The foregoing has only one purpose: to encourage the reader to respect his body. This amazing instrument is what we have the effrontery to call "a clumsy oaf." Reflect on the silent intelligence of your body, and the arrogant mistrust we have of Self 2 will begin to dissolve. With it will dissolve the many self-instructions that occupy the unconcentrated mind.

Trust Thyself

There will be little hope of getting Self 1 and Self 2 together without developing trust between them. As long as Self 1 is ignorant of the true capabilities of Self 2, he is likely to mistrust it. It is the mistrust of Self 2 which causes both the interference called "trying too hard" and that of too much self-instruction. The first results in using too many muscles, the second in mental distraction and lack of concentration. Clearly, the new relationship to be established with ourselves must be based on the maxim "Trust thyself."

What does "Trust thyself" mean on the tennis court? It doesn't mean positive thinking—for example, expecting that you are going to hit an ace on every serve. Trusting your body in tennis means *letting* your body hit the ball. The key word is *let*. You trust in the competence of your body and its brain, and you *let* it swing the racket. Self 1 stays out of it. But though this is very simple, it does not mean that it is easy.

In some ways the relationship between Self 1 and Self 2 is analogous to the relationship between parent and child. Some parents have a hard time letting their children do something when they believe that they themselves know better how it should be done. But the trusting and loving parent lets the child perform his own actions, even to the extent of making mistakes, because he trusts the child to learn from them.

Letting it happen is not *making* it happen. It is not trying hard. It is not controlling your shots. These are all the actions of Self 1, who takes things into his own hands because he mistrusts Self 2. This is what produces tight muscles, rigid swings, awkward movements, gritted teeth and tense cheek muscles. The results are mis-hit balls and a lot of frustration. Often when we are rallying we trust our bodies and let it happen because the ego-mind tells itself that it doesn't really count. But once the game begins, watch Self 1 take over; at the crucial point he starts to doubt whether Self 2 will perform well. The more important the point, the more Self 1 will try to control the shot, and this is exactly when tightening up occurs. The results are almost always frustrating.

Let's take a closer look at this tightening process, because it is a phenomenon which takes place in every athlete in every sport. Anatomy tells us that muscles are two-way mechanisms; that is, a given muscle is either relaxed or contracted. It can't be partially contracted any more than a light switch can be partially off. The difference between holding our racket loosely or tightly is in the *number* of muscles which are contracted. How many and which muscles are actually needed to hit a fast serve? No one knows, but if the conscious mind *thinks* it does and tries to control those muscles, it will inevitably use muscles that aren't needed. When more than necessary are used, not only is there a waste of energy, but certain tightened muscles interfere with the need of other muscles to stretch. Thinking that it has to use a lot of muscle to hit as hard as it wants to, Self 1 will initiate the use of muscles in the shoulder, forearm, wrist and even face which will actually *impede* the force of the swing.

If you have a racket handy, hold it and try this experiment. (If you don't have a racket, grab any movable object, or just grab the air with your hand.) Tighten up the muscles in your wrist and see how fast you can snap your racket. Then release the muscles in your wrist and see how fast it will snap. Clearly, a loose wrist is more flexible. When serving, power is generated by the flexible snap of the wrist. If you try to hit hard intentionally, you are likely to tighten the wrist muscles, slow down the snap of your wrist, and thereby lose power. Furthermore, the entire stroke will be rigid, and balance will be difficult to maintain. This is how Self 1 interferes with the wisdom of the body. (As you can imagine, a stiff-wristed serve will not meet the expectations of the server. Consequently he is likely to try even harder next time, tightening more muscles, and becoming more and more frustrated and exhausted—and, I might add, increasing the risk of tennis elbow.)

Fortunately, most children learn to walk before they can be told how to by their parents. As a result, children not only learn how to walk very well, but they gain confidence in the natural learning process which operates within them. Mothers observe their children's efforts with love and interest, and if they are wise, without much interference. If we could treat our tennis games as we do a child learning to walk, we would make amazing progress. When the child loses his balance and falls, the mother doesn't condemn it for being clumsy. She doesn't even feel bad about it; she simply notices the event and perhaps gives a word or gesture of encouragement. Consequently, a child's progress in learning to walk is never hindered by the idea that he is uncoordinated.

Why shouldn't a beginning player treat his backhand as a loving mother would her child? The trick is not to *identify* with the backhand. If you view an erratic backhand as a reflection of who you are, you will be upset. But you are not your backhand any more than a parent is his child. If a mother identifies with every fall of her child and takes personal pride in its every success, her self-image will be as unstable as her child's balance. She finds stability when she realizes that she is not her child, and watches it with love and interest—but as a separate being.

This same kind of detached interest is what is necessary to let your tennis game develop naturally. Remember that you are not your tennis game. You are not your body. Trust the body to learn and to play, as you would trust another person to do a job, and in a short time it will perform beyond your expectations. *Let* the flower grow.

The preceding theory should be tested and not taken on faith. Toward the end of the chapter there are several experiments that will give you a chance to experience the difference between *making* yourself do something, and *letting* it happen. I suggest that you also devise your own experiments to discover just how much you are willing to trust yourself, both when rallying and when under pressure.

Programming Self 2

At this point it may have occurred to the reader to ask, "How can I just 'let a forehand happen' if I've never learned how to hit one in the first place? Don't I need someone to tell me how to do it? If I've never played tennis before, can I just go out on the court and 'let it happen'"? The answer is: if your body knows how to hit a forehand, then just *let it happen;* if it doesn't, then *let it learn.*

The actions of Self 2 are based on information it has stored in its memory of past actions of itself or of the observed actions of others. A player who has never held a racket in his hand needs to let the ball hit the strings a few times before Self 2 learns how far away the center of the racket is from the hand holding it. Every time you hit a ball, whether correctly or incorrectly, the computer memory of Self 2 is picking up valuable information and storing it away for future use. As one practices, Self 2 refines and extends the information in its memory bank. All the time it is learning such things as how high a ball bounces when hit at varying speeds and varying spins; how fast a ball falls and how fast if comes up off the court; and where it should be met to direct it to different parts of the court. It remembers every action it makes and the results of every action, depending on the degree of your attention and alertness. So the important thing for a beginning player to remember is to allow the natural learning process to take place and to forget about stroke-by-stroke self-instructions. The results will be surprising.

Having said this, let me add that Self 1 does have some role in this process. He *can* function in a cooperative way, though the role is a more humble one than he usually prefers. The main job of Self 1, the conscious ego-mind, is to set goals, that is, to communicate to Self 2 what he wants from it and then to let Self 2 do it. If you walked onto the court without a goal and let Self 2 do what it wanted, you might end up hitting all the balls over the fence as hard as you could and have a great time. But if your intention is to keep the balls within the lines, that goal must be communicated to Self 2. This communication can be accomplished in a natural and effortless way, but if there is the usual communication gap and mistrust between the two selves, the learning process will be slow and awkward. Let me illustrate with an example which demonstrates the easy and hard ways of learning.

When I was twelve years old, I was sent to dancing school, where I was taught the waltz, fox trot and other steps known only to the darker ages of man. We were told, "Put your right foot here and your left foot there, then bring them together. Now shift your weight to your left foot, turn," and so forth. The steps were not complicated, but it was weeks before I was dancing without the need to play back the tape in my head: "Put your left foot here, right foot there, turn, one, two, three; one, two, three." I would think out each step, command myself to do it, and then execute it. I was barely aware there was a girl in my arms, and it was weeks before I was able to handle a conversation while dancing.

This is the way most of us teach ourselves the footwork and strokes of tennis. But it's such a slow and painful way! Contrast it with the way the modern twelve-year-old learns to dance. He goes to a party one night, sees his friends doing the Monkey, the Jerk, and the Swim, and comes home having mastered them all. Yet these dances are infinitely more complex than the fox trot. Just imagine the size of the instruction manual required to put into words each of the movements involved in doing the Monkey! It would require a Ph.D. in physical education and a full semester to learn these dances "by the book." But a kid who may be failing math and English learns them effortlessly in a single night.

How does he do this? First, by simply *watching.* He doesn't think about what he is seeing—how the left shoulder lifts a bit while the head jerks forward and the right foot twists. He simply absorbs *visually* the image in front of him. This image completely bypasses the ego-mind, and seems to be fed directly to the body, for in a few minutes the kid is on the floor doing movements very similar to those he was watching. Now he is *feeling* how it is to imitate those images. He repeats the process a few times, first looking, then feeling, and soon is dancing effortlessly—totally "with it." If the next day he is asked by his sister how to do the Monkey he'll say, "I don't know . . . like this . . . see?" Ironically, he thinks he doesn't know how to do the dance because he can't explain it in words, while most of us who learn tennis through verbal instruction can explain in great detail how the ball should be hit but have trouble doing it.

To Self 2, a picture is worth a thousand words. It learns by watching the actions of others, as well as by performing actions itself. Almost all tennis players have experienced playing over their heads after watching championship tennis on television. The benefits to your game come not from analyzing the strokes of top players, but from concentrating without thinking and simply letting yourself absorb the images before you. Then, the next time you play, you may find that certain important intangibles such as timing, anticipation and sense of confidence are greatly improved, all without conscious effort or control.

Programming Self 2's Computer

Up to this point we have discussed the need to quiet Self 1, to slow down his judging and controlling activities. It may have sounded as if we wanted to get rid of Self 1 entirely. But the conscious self does have a valid role in learning and playing tennis. By assuming his proper role and letting go of his improper ones he can greatly speed the learning process and help Self 2 reach the limits of its abilities.

Learning tennis without the help of Self 1 would be like learning tennis on an island where the game had never been heard of. If the rules of tennis were introduced to such an island, and courts were built and equipment provided, eventually the strokes used by the island players would come to resemble closely those which we now generally consider "proper." The speed with which these strokes would be learned would depend on the extent to which Self 2 was left to its own resources—that is, the extent to which Self 1 refrained from interfering with the natural learning process. But this learning would take a great deal longer than it would in a society where there were plenty of models of effective tennis for one to learn from. In a tennis-playing society, Self 1 can assume an important role by frequently exposing Self 2 to models of high-caliber tennis. In this way, Self 1 programs the computer memory bank of Self 2 with valuable information which might take it a long time to develop on its own.

55

The remainder of this chapter will discuss three basic methods of programming Self 2. By this I simply mean communicating to Self 2 what you want from it. The primary role of Self 1 is to set goals for Self 2, then to *let* Self 2 perform. It is basic to good communications that we use the most suitable language. If Mr. A wishes to make sure of getting his message across to Mr. B, he will, if he can, use Mr. B's native tongue. What is the native language of Self 2? Certainly not words! Words were not learned by Self 2 until several years after birth. No, the native tongue of Self 2 is imagery: sensory images. Movements are learned through visual and feeling images. So the three methods of programming I will discuss all involve communicating goal-oriented messages to Self 2 by images and "feelmages."

Programming for Results

Many students of tennis are too stroke-conscious and not attentive enough to results. Such players are aware of *how* they stroke the ball, but unconcerned with *where* it is actually going. It is often helpful for these players to shift their attention from means to ends. Here is an example.

During a group lesson with five women, I asked each player what one change she would most like to make in her game. The first woman, Sally, wanted to work on her forehand, which she said "had really been terrible lately." When I asked her what she didn't like about her forehand, she replied, "Well, I take my racket back too late and too high, and I roll it over too much on the follow-through; also I take my eye off the ball a lot, and I don't think I step into it very well." It was clear that if I were to give her instruction on each element she mentioned, I would start and end the lesson with her.

So I asked Sally what she felt about the results of her forehand, and she replied, "It goes too shallow and doesn't have much power." Now we had something we could work with. I told her that I imagined her body (Self 2) already knew how to hit the ball deep and with more power, and that if it didn't, it would learn very quickly. I suggested that she imagine the arc the ball would have to take to land deep in the court, noticing how high over the net it would pass, and to hold that image in her mind for several seconds. Then, before hitting some balls, I said, "Don't *try* to hit the ball deep. Just ask Self 2 to do it and let it happen. If the ball continues to fall shallow, don't make any conscious effort to correct. Simply let go and see what happens."

The third ball Sally hit landed a foot inside the base line. Of the next twenty, fifteen landed in the back quarter of the court and did so with increasing force behind them. As she hit, the other four women and I could see all the elements she had mentioned changing appreciably and naturally; her backswing lowered, her follow-through flattened, and she began flowing into the ball with balance and confidence. When she was finished hitting, I asked her what changes she had made, and she replied, "I didn't make any. I just imagined the ball passing two feet over the net and landing near the base line, and it did!" She was both delighted and surprised.

The changes which Sally made in her forehand lay in the fact that she gave Self 2 a clear visual image of the *results* she desired. Then she told her body in effect, "Do whatever you have to do to go there." All she had to do was *let it happen.*

Programming for results is the most useful method of communicating with Self 2 when playing a match. Once you are competing it is too late to work on your strokes, but it is possible to hold in your mind the image of where you want the ball to go and then allow the body to do what is necessary to hit it there. It is essential here to trust Self 2. Self 1 must stay relaxed, refraining from giving "how-to-do-it" instructions and from any effort to control the stroke. As Self 1 learns to let go, a growing confidence in the ability of Self 2 emerges.

Programming for Form

It is sometimes useful to be able to make a deliberate change in one or more elements of a given stroke when simple nonjudgmental attention and programming by results both fail to produce the desired results. Then it is appropriate to use another kind of programming—programming for form. (This process will be discussed in greater detail in Chapter 6, "Changing Habits: A New Way of Learning.")

In brief, the process is very similar to programming for results. Suppose, for example, that you are consistently rolling your racket over on the follow-through, and the habit continues despite all efforts to change it. First you must give Self 2 a very clear image of what you are asking it to do. This can best be done by holding your racket in front of you in a proper follow-through position and looking at it with undivided attention for several seconds. You may feel foolish, thinking that you already know the proper fellow-through, but it is vital to give Self 2 an image to imitate. Having done this, it might also be useful to shut your eyes and imagine as clearly as possible your entire forehand with the racket staying flat throughout the swing. Then, before hitting any balls, swing your racket several times, letting the racket stay flat and allowing yourself to experience how it feels to swing in this new way. Once you start to hit balls, it is important not to try and keep your racket flat. You have asked Self 2 to keep it flat, so *let it happen!* Once having programmed the body, Self 2's only role is to be still and observe the results in a detached manner. Let me stress again that it is important not to make any conscious effort to keep the racket flat. If after a few strokes the racket does not conform to the image you gave Self 2, then program and let your body swing your racket, making sure Self 2 isn't giving it the slightest assistance. Don't *try* to make this experiment work; if you do, Self 1 will get involved and you won't really know if Self 2 is hitting the ball unassisted or not.

Two Experiments

It is important not only to understand intellectually the difference between *letting* it happen and *making* it happen, but to *experience* the difference. To experience the difference is to know the difference. To this end, let me suggest two experiments.

The first involves trying to hit a stationary target with a tennis ball. Place a tennis-ball can in the backhand corner of one of the service courts. Then figure out how you should swing your racket in order to hit the can. Think about how high to toss the ball, about the proper angle of your racket at impact, the proper weight flow, and so forth. Now aim at the can and attempt to hit it. If you miss, try again. If you hit it, try to repeat whatever you did so that you can hit it again. If you follow this procedure for a few minutes, you will experience what I mean by "trying hard" and *making* yourself serve.

After you have absorbed this experience, move the can to the backhand corner of the other service court for the second half of the experiment. This time stand on the base line, breathe deeply a few times and relax. Look at the can. Then visualize the path of the ball from your racket to the can. See the ball hitting the can right on the label. If you like, shut your eyes and imagine yourself serving and the ball hitting the can. Do this several times. If in your imagination the ball misses the can, that's all right; repeat the image a few times until the ball hits the target. Now, take no thought of how you should hit the ball. Don't *try* to hit the target. *Ask* your body, Self 2, to do whatever is necessary to hit the can, then let it do it. Exercise no control; correct for no imagined bad habits. Having programmed yourself with the desired flight of the ball, simply trust your body to do it. When you toss the ball up, focus your attention on its seams, then let the serve serve itself.

The ball will either hit or miss the target. Notice exactly where it lands. You should free yourself from any emotional reaction to success or failure; simply know your goal and take objective interest in the results. Then serve again. If you have missed the can, don't be surprised and don't try to correct for your error. This is most important. Again focus your attention on the can; then let the serve serve itself. If you faithfully do not *try* to hit the can, and do not attempt to correct for your misses, but put full confidence in your body and its computer, you will soon see that the serve is correcting itself. You will experience that there really is a Self 2 who is acting and learning without being told what to do. Observe this process; observe your body making the changes necessary in order to come nearer and nearer to the can. Of course, Self 1 is very tricky and it is most difficult to keep him from interfering a little, but if you quiet him a bit, you will begin to see Self 2 at work, and you will be as amazed as I have been at what it can do, and how effortlessly.

The second experiment I would recommend in order to experience the reality of Self 2 begins with picking some change you would like to make in one of your strokes. For instance, choose a bad habit that you have been trying unsuccessfully to alter. Then on the court, ask a friend to throw you twenty balls and try to correct the habit. Tell him what you are trying to do and ask him to observe if it is correcting. Try hard; try the way you are used to in attempting to change a habit. Experience this kind of trying. Observe how you feel if you fail. Also note whether you feel awkward or tight. Now try to practice your corrected stroke while rallying. Then see what happens when you play a match.

Next, pick another habit you would like to change, or even the same one. (If the habit has not been corrected by your first efforts, it would be interesting to work on the same one.) Ask your friend to throw you five or ten balls. During this, make no attempt to change your stroke; simply observe it. Don't analyze it, just *observe* it carefully; experience where your racket is at all times. Changes may occur while you are merely observing your stroke nonjudgmentally, but if you feel further correction is needed, then "program for form." Show yourself exactly what you want Self 2 to do. Give it a clear visual image, moving your racket slowly in the desired path, and let yourself watch it very closely. Then repeat the process, but this time *feel* exactly what it's like to move your racket in this new manner.

Having programmed yourself with an image and a feeling, you are ready to hit some balls. Now focus your eyes and mind on the seams of the ball and *let it happen.* Then *observe* what happened. Once again, don't analyze; simply see how close Self 2 came to doing what you wanted it to. If your racket didn't follow exactly the path you had programmed, then reprogram and let the stroke happen again. Continue this process, letting Self 1 relax more and more with each ball. Soon you will see that Self 2 can be trusted. Long-standing habits can be altered in a few moments. After twenty balls or so, ask your friend to rally again with you. Be sure you don't try to make this experiment work by attempting to do it "right" when playing; merely continue to observe the precise part of your swing that is changing. Watch it with detachment and care as you would watch someone else's stroke. Watch it, and it will change quite effortlessly by its own smooth process.

Perhaps this seems too good to be true. I can only suggest that you experiment and see for yourself.

More needs to be said about this art of changing habits because it is what so many players spend so much time and money on in lessons, but before undertaking a fuller description of this art, let's discuss a third method of programming Self 2.

Programming by Identity

In the last chapter, I pointed out how the process of judgment often feeds on and extends itself until a strong negative self-image has formed. One begins believing that he is not a good tennis player and then acts this role, never allowing himself anything but glimpses of his true capabilities. Most players hypnotize themselves into acting the roles of much worse players than they actually are, but interesting results can often be achieved by doing a little role-playing of a different kind.

"Programming by identity" is a phrase to describe this other kind of role-playing. When introducing this idea, I usually say something like this: "Imagine that I am the director of a television series. Knowing that you are an actor that plays tennis, I ask if you would like to do a bit part as a top-flight tennis player. I assure you that you needn't worry about hitting the ball out or into the net because the camera will only be focused on you and will not follow the ball. What I'm mainly interested in is that you adapt professional mannerisms, and that you swing your racket with supreme self-assurance. Above all, your face must express no self-doubt. You should look as if you are hitting every ball exactly where you want to. Really get into the role, hit as hard as you like and ignore where the ball is actually going."

When a player succeeds in forgetting himself and really acts out his assumed role, remarkable changes in his game often take place; if you don't mind puns, you might even say that the changes are dramatic. As long as he is able to stay in this role he experiences a style that he may not have known was in his repertoire.

There is an important distinction between this kind of role-playing and what is normally called positive thinking. In the latter, you are telling yourself that you are as good as Ken Rosewall, while in the former you are not trying to convince yourself that you are any better than you believe you are. You are quite consciously playing a role, but in the process, you may become more aware of the range of your true capabilities.

The process is similar to the one that occurs when a sweet thirteen-year-old high school girl who has never been kissed is asked to play the part of the *femme fatale* in a school play. As she gets into the role, she is almost as astonished as the audience at how comfortably she can act the part.

Experimenting with Role-Playing

After they have played tennis for a year or so, most people fall into a particular pattern of play from which they seldom depart. Some adopt a defensive style; they spare no effort to retrieve every ball, lob often, hit deep into the opponent's court, and seldom hit the ball hard or go for a winner. The defensive player waits for his opponent to make an error and wears him down by degrees with endless patience. Some Italian clay-court players are the prototype for this style.

The opposite of this is the offensive style adopted by some great and would-be great American players. In its extreme form the ball is hit for a winner every time. Every serve is designed to be an ace, every return of serve a clean passing shot, while volleys and overheads are all aimed to land within one or two inches of the lines.

A third common pattern is what might be called the "formal" style of play. Players in this category don't care so much where their ball goes as long as they look good stroking it. They would rather be seen using flawless form than winning the match.

In contrast, there is the competitive style of the player who will do anything to win. He runs hard and hits hard or soft, depending on what seems to bother his opponent most, and uses gamesmanship to the hilt.

One final style worth mentioning is that of the detached Buddhist. He plays with perfect serenity, aware of everything but attached to nothing; that is, even though he makes great effort, he seems unconcerned with the results of his actions. Always alert, he shows no tension even on match point.

Having outlined these basic styles to a group of players, I often suggest that as an experiment they adopt the style that seems most unlike the one they have previously adopted. I also suggest that they act the role of a good player, no matter what style they have chosen. Besides being a lot of fun, this kind of role-playing can greatly increase a player's range. The defensive player learns that he can hit winners; the aggressive one finds that he can also be stylish. I have found that when players break their habitual patterns, they can greatly extend the limits of their own style and explore subdued aspects of their personality.

Letting go of judgments, the art of programming with images and "letting it happen" are three of the basic skills involved in the Inner Game. Before going on to the fourth and most important inner skill, that of concentration, I will devote one chapter to a discussion of *external* technique. Once you learn to let Self 2 do the learning, relatively few instructions on stroke and footwork are needed.

5. Master Tips

The preceding chapters put heavy emphasis on the importance of quieting the mind by letting go of mental self-instructions and trusting the body to do what comes most naturally. The purpose of these chapters was not to disparage stroke technique in learning tennis but to prepare the way for the proper use of such knowledge. There is nothing wrong with knowing that a firm wrist will tend to increase the consistency of one's backhand, but if, on learning this, the player persists in telling himself to keep his wrist firm before every shot, fluid tennis will evade him. Thinking himself into doing everything by the book, he will experience the awkwardness, inconsistency and frustration all too familiar to most players.

A most important lesson can be learned by watching the way animals teach their children basic skills. Not long ago I was walking through the San Diego Zoo and came upon a pool just in time to see a mother hippopotamus giving her newborn child what appeared to be its first swimming lesson. At the deep end of the pool one hippo was floating with just his nose appearing above the surface. Soon he submerged and sank to the bottom, where he rested for about twenty seconds before pushing off with his hind legs and rising again toward the surface. Then I watched the mother hippo, which had been nursing her baby in the sun, get up and begin to push it toward the pond with her snout. When the child toppled in, it sank like a rock to the bottom and stayed there. Mother sauntered casually to the shallow end of the pool and waded in. About twenty seconds later she reached the baby and began to lift it upward with her nose, sending it toward the surface. There the young student gasped a breath and sank again. Once again the mother repeated the process, but this time moved off to the deeper end of the pool, somehow knowing that her role in the learning process was finished. The baby hippo inhaled on the surface and sank again to the bottom, but after some time he pushed himself toward the air with his own hind legs. Then he repeated his new skill again and again.

It seemed to me that the mother knew that somehow her child already knew what she was teaching it, and her role was simply to give nudging encouragement so that the baby's behavior would fall into a pattern whose form was already imprinted within it.

I like to think that the same holds true for tennis strokes: that the perfect strokes are already within us waiting to be discovered, and that the role of the pro is to give nudging encouragement. One reason I like to think this is that when I and my students think of strokes as being *discovered* rather than manufactured, they seem to learn the game much faster and without frustration.

Instructions properly given and used can help a player discover his groove faster than if he were left on his own. But beware of too many instructions, and beware of mistaking them for the groove itself. No single chapter could describe all the elements of each of the three major strokes. A moment ago I noted on a piece of scratch paper some of the important components of the standing forehand; there were over fifty. If it had included common instructions on things *not* to do, the list would have grown to over two hundred. The best advice I can give to the student of stroke technique is *keep it simple, keep it natural.*

Master tips refers to certain key elements of a stroke which, if done properly, tend to cause many other elements to be done properly. By discovering the groove of these key elements of behavior there is little need to concern yourself with scores of secondary details. Please do not take these suggestions as commands with which to bludgeon your body into "right" behavior, but as gentle nudges meant to help you find your own most natural and effective way of hitting a tennis ball. Few of the following instructions are original, but each has been tested, and its merit proven.

Before beginning, let me simplify the external problem facing the tennis player. He faces only two requirements for winning any given point: each ball must be hit over the net and into his opponent's court. The sole aim of stroke technique is to fulfill these two requirements with consistency and with enough pace and accuracy to keep pressure on one's opponent. Keeping it simple, let's look at the dynamics for hitting forehand and backhand ground strokes both over the net and into the court.

Ground Strokes

Hitting the ball over the net wouldn't be difficult if it weren't for the requirement that the ball come back down again in the court. What besides gravity makes a ball come down? How to keep the ball from going out of the court is the greatest technical problem involved in hitting ground strokes. Here it may be of interest to understand something about a certain law of physics which governs the flight of a spinning tennis ball. Although it is not essential to understand the physics of the matter, it may help in understanding why ground strokes are hit the way they are.

Some may remember from their high school physics class the name of a Swiss mathematician named Daniel Bernoulli and his namesake, Bernoulli's Principle. This theorem states that in any horizontally moving fluid the pressure increases as the velocity decreases. Got it? The concept may grow more interesting when seen in relation to a tennis ball. Air is a fluid that moves horizontally in respect to a tennis ball moving from one side of the net to the other. The pressure of that air on the ball affects its flight. When the ball is hit with topspin—that is, with the top of the ball spinning in the same direction as the flight of the ball—the relative velocity of air will be least at the top of the ball. Thus, according to Bernoulli's Principle, the pressure at the top of the ball will be greatest. This higher pressure tends to push the ball toward the ground. Conversely, when a ball is hit with underspin—with the bottom of the ball moving in the same direction as its flight—the greater pressure at the bottom tends to keep the ball from dropping.

Even if you didn't fully understand the theory, I recommend an experiment if you aren't already aware of the effect of spin on the flight of the ball. First hit several balls hard with heavy underspin. (Do this by taking your backswing above the level of the ball and slicing down through it, finishing with your racket below the level of impact with the ball.) Watch the ball's flight carefully. Not only will it tend to float, but if you hit with enough underspin, you may even see it rise above the level of its original trajectory.

Next, hit several balls with topspin. Topspin is best achieved by taking a low backswing and finishing with a follow-through at shoulder level or higher. In this way, the racket brushes the ball upward. If the racket face has been flat throughout the stroke, you will notice that the balls first tend to rise, and then to dive down toward the court. Now, hitting with medium to heavy topspin, try to hit the ball out. If you aim one or two feet over the net, you will experience how difficult it is to hit a topspin ball out. The more topspin, the more difficult it is. It's fun to find a way to stroke the ball which makes it hard to hit out!

The clear lesson to be learned is that topspin balls can be hit quite high over the net without going out of the court. This allows you a wide margin for error and increases consistency. On the other hand, a stroke hit with underspin must be hit lower to the net to be kept in the court, thus increasing the chances of error.

A smooth and low backswing is the key to achieving topspin, and is usually the first component of a ground stroke which should be mastered. The reason is simple: most of the bad habits which players accumulate in their ground strokes are caused by their jury-rigged attempts to keep their shots from sailing out. Usually the first thing a player will try is rolling his racket over after hitting the ball. Unfortunately, this may work a few times, encouraging the repetition of the behavior. But inconsistency soon sets in because of the difficulty of knowing just how much and just when to turn the racket face. Next the player may try shortening his follow-through, or not stepping into the ball. Both these devices deprive the stroke of power and don't help much in keeping the ball in the court. Common sense may then dictate taking the racket back higher and leveling out the swing; surely this will keep the ball lower. But though the ball may be closer to the ground as it passes over the net, it will lack topspin and tend to sail out — exactly the opposite of the intended result. The next common step is to take the racket still higher on the backswing, and soon the player is hitting the ball with underspin and has a very small margin for error.

Contrary to common sense, it is a *low* backswing which helps to keep ground strokes from flying out. If a player takes his racket back enough below the level of the ball to produce medium topspin, he frees himself from the need to complicate his stroke with other devices for controlling the ball. Furthermore, when he discovers how difficult it is to hit a topspin ball out, he begins to hit strongly with confidence, stepping into the ball without fear that it will sail out.

In short, when hitting ground strokes, allow your body to turn sideways to the net, drawing the racket back below the level of the ball (between the knee and waist for a waist-high ball), pausing when it is about perpendicular to the base line. Then, keeping the racket as flat as you would if hitting it with your hand, let it swing forward to meet the ball at a point even with your front foot, and then follow through to about shoulder level. Consider the racket an extension of your arm, and the racket face your hand. Hit the ball as if you were hitting your hand. Let the stroke be natural; let it remain simple. If you do, you won't get involved with varying the face of your racket, with flicks of the wrist, or with other complications that make for inconsistent strokes. Remember: *simplicity is the key to consistency.*

Even if you develop perfect footwork and racket work, it will be impossible to achieve consistency, power or accuracy if you don't discover a sense of timing. Timing is a complicated matter, so one shouldn't *think* about it. However, one should *pay attention* to it. For instance, hit several balls while giving close attention to where your racket head is at the moment the ball lands on your side of the court. Don't try to take your racket back early; simply observe how you naturally take it back in relation to the oncoming ball. Many beginners wait for the ball to bounce before beginning their swing; as a result they are usually rushed. Some players have trained themselves always to be prepared by taking their racket back as quickly as possible; these players often lose their natural sense of rhythm and find themselves waiting with their racket back before hitting.

Next hit a few balls while observing where your racket *meets* the ball. Don't try to do what you think is "right"; merely observe where, in relation to your front foot, your racket meets the ball. Note this as precisely as you can. Perhaps at first the point of impact will vary, but before long it will tend to become consistent as you pay attention to it. For most people it comes to feel natural and best when the ball is met about even with the front foot on the forehand, and a few inches ahead of the front foot on the backhand.

Summary

1. **Backswing:** Exactly where do you place your racket head on the backswing? What happens to the face of the racket?

2. **Impact:** Can you feel the racket imparting topspin to the ball?

3. **Follow-through:** Where does your racket finish? In what direction? Is the face flat?

4. **Footwork:** Are you flowing into the ball with confidence? What is your weight doing at the moment of impact? Do you retreat as the ball approaches? What kind of base do you hit from?

5. **Timing:** Where is your racket head (level and direction) at the moment the ball bounces? Where do you make contact with the ball relative to your front foot?

Remember to use the above checkpoints not to tell yourself how to hit the ball, but as points of observation. Simply pay attention to each of these elements one at a time, and allow the process to bring you to the most natural and effective way for *you* to hit forehands and backhands.

The Volley

To understand the volley it is helpful to take a good look at the situation that presents itself when you are standing at the net in volley position. From near the net it is possible to hit almost any spot in the court and at angles that are geometrically impossible when hitting from the backcourt. There is no way an opponent can cover all the shots that can be hit from the net. In addition, since you are almost twice as close to your opponent than usual, he has only half the time to react to the shot you hit. Hence, when you are at net, you are in an offensive position with many opportunities. The closer to the net you meet the ball, the more opportunities you have. Realize also that you too have only half the normal time to respond to your opponent's shot, so be very alert!

This fact governs the two cardinal principles of effective volleying. First, do not take a backswing; you seldom have time. Secondly, *meet the ball as far out in front of you as you comfortably can.* It's almost impossible to hit a volley too early. In front of you is where the ball can best be seen; in front of you is where you have the best angles; in front of you is where you will find power in your volley. If you really want to hit the volley in front of you, you will find that the most effective footwork and racket work will come into being quite automatically. It will also require of you the alertness that is indispensable to effective volleying. (See Chapter 9, "Concentration.")

The greatest problem most players have with the volley is that they simply do not enjoy the stroke enough. To volley well, you must really *want* to. Then you will become alert, will anticipate each ball, and will step forward to meet it. But if you have the idea that you don't volley well, you are apt to hesitate, and if you fear it, you are apt to step back instead of forward.

Volleying can be the most exciting part of tennis, and the most fun. If you do not find this so, I recommend a little practice of the art of programming by identity (Chapter 4). Do some role-playing, acting the part of a confident, quick volleyer. Get into the role, and if you give it a chance, the necessary behavior will follow your assumed attitude.

Try the space theory of the volley. As you are about to volley, not only watch the ball but be aware of the top of the net. See the space between the ball and the top of the net extending as a rectangular corridor to the court and punch the ball through that space. The higher the ball is over the net, the more space you have to punch it through, so get to the ball early. Let yourself be quick; let yourself punch the ball through the space and down into the court.

However, sometimes it is impossible to reach the ball before it has dipped below the level of the net. In this case you have to bend your knees, watch the ball, be aware of the top of the net, and let yourself be firm, yet more delicate. Compare how it is to hit a volley from below with hitting it from above; this will increase your incentive to meet the ball before it has time to drop. Never wait for the ball to come to you when at net; ask your body to spring forward. Be very alert.

The Serve

Compared with the other strokes of tennis, the serve is the most complicated. Both arms are involved in the stroke, and your serving arm is making simultaneous movements in the shoulder, elbow and wrist. The movements of the serve are much too complicated for Self 1 to learn and to try to apply. Let Self 2 watch some professionals serve. Stan Smith's serve is an excellent model for men, and Billy Jean King's for women. Watch these serves carefully, then imitate the motions and rhythm with your own racket. If you are watching TV, practice right in front of your set.

If you find this imitation difficult, perhaps you are thinking too hard about it. One way to get into the natural motion of the serve is to experience how much serving is like throwing. Throw a tennis ball over the net with your serving arm. Then repeat the motion very slowly, experiencing the movement of your arm. If you have an old racket, go to an open area of grass and wind up and throw your racket high into the air with an overhand motion. The way one throws is usually the most natural way to serve.

The *key* position in both throwing and serving is with the elbow high, and with the racket dropping down your back. Realize that as in throwing, most of the power of the serve comes from the snap of the wrist. Most people serve with less power than they are capable of because they do not allow the wrist to snap fully.

There are two common reasons for this. One is that the player is often trying so hard to hit the ball with force that he grips his racket too hard. Grip your racket handle with all your strength and see how inflexible your wrist becomes. The racket must be held firmly, but not so tightly that your wrist becomes inflexible. Grip your handle as you would a bird: not so tightly that you squeeze the life from it, and not so loosely that it will escape.

The second common reason for limited wrist snap is the use of a grip that locks the wrist. The closer you are to a backhand grip, the more wrist snap is possible. People who serve with a Western forehand grip will find they can rotate their wrist only 90 degrees. Their racket extends back a little farther than to a vertical angle relative to the court and snaps through a 90-degree arc until the racket is parallel to the court. With an Eastern forehand grip—that is, with the "V" between thumb and forefinger centered on top of the racket—most wrists are able to cock back an additional 20 degrees and to follow through fifteen degrees below the horizontal. With a backhand grip, as much as an additional 30 degrees of arc is possible. The greater the arc of wrist snap possible, the greater the force that can be generated, so allow your wrist to be flexible and swing in its greatest possible arc.

Beginners may not find it a simple matter to begin serving with the backhand grip. I would recommend that they start with an Eastern forehand grip and *slowly* edge over toward the backhand grip as it grows more comfortable. Allow at least a year to complete the change.

A consistent toss is indispensable to achieving a consistent serve. If the body has to swing differently on every serve to go after tosses which vary in height and placement, how can it develop a uniform motion and rhythm? To toss the ball consistently, let your movement be as smooth as an elevator. Hold the ball in the cushions of your first three fingers, drop your arm to your leg, then lift it as slowly and evenly as an elevator. Release the ball at the top floor by opening your fingers. Ask your body to lift the ball just a little higher than the full extension of your arm and racket. Ask yourself to place the ball slightly in front and to the outside of your front foot. Visualize the spot in the air where you want the ball to be tossed, and then *ask* yourself to put it there. Don't try to correct faulty tosses—and don't hit faulty tosses. Simply reprogram and let your body do it. Self 2 will make all the necessary corrections.

The problem of rhythm in the serve is complicated because the two arms must move in coordination with each other. Watch Stan Smith serve. Starting with his right and left hands together, both drop at the same time. The right arm drops down until the racket is just past the vertical with the court, and at the same time the left arm drops down toward his left thigh. Then both arms rise together at approximately the same rate of speed. Moving the arms together in this manner achieves a natural rhythm and allows for an unrushed yet powerful motion. Many players fail to take the tossing arm down to the leg, and are therefore forced either to move the serving arm very fast, or to throw the ball very high to give the serving arm time to complete its full swing.

When serving, don't simply aim for the court; get into the habit of aiming for a particular spot. Imagine clearly the entire path of the ball, noticing exactly which square in the net the ball should pass over and at what height. Don't worry whether you hit your spot, but if you give your computer a bull's-eye to aim at, your percentage of faults will decrease appreciably. Remember: after aiming for your spot, don't *try* to hit it. Let Self 2 take care of that. Self 1 picks the spot and then simply observes how Self 2 performs. Eliminate ego involvement in your serve and you will eliminate frustration. Eliminate frustration, and you will find yourself serving accurately.

The Overhead Smash

The overhead smash is even more complex than the serve, but the motion is very similar. I have only a few things to say about the smash other than that again you should try to imitate the stroke and rhythm of an experienced player.

The smash is similar to the serve, the only difference being that your opponent has tossed the ball up for you. Usually it is high, and far from where you are standing. This creates a difficult problem of timing which only your built-in computer is capable of solving. How fast is the ball coming down? When must I begin my swing in order to meet the ball at the highest point? Self 2 can only solve this problem with consistency if it has experienced a lot of balls dropping toward it from different heights and trajectories, so practice is required. Let your computer learn. Don't jam its system by trying to figure it out yourself, or by getting discouraged if you miss a few. Watch the ball carefully; watch its seams spinning above you. It's a good idea to let your left hand point toward the ball as it falls. Make the timing easier by taking an abbreviated backswing. Take your racket directly behind your back and keep it cocked and ready for the right moment to swing through. Let your body decide when the time is right; it will learn quickly if you let it.

You can also help yourself hit decisive smashes by never being surprised when your opponent lobs. If you expect him to lob, you will have a split-second more to get into position. As soon as you see a lob, turn sidewise and take your racket back; then let your body move quickly under the ball, skipping backward or forward in a sidewise position. Let your body be aggressive. *Smash* the ball; don't pat it back. There is something in Self 2 which wants to let out all the stops. The overhead smash is one of the few strokes it can hit with abandon, without worry about hitting it too hard, so let it. But don't try to help it hit hard by using *all* your arm muscles. Self 2 knows which muscles to use. Let it experiment, and you'll find yourself hitting smashes that don't come back. Trust yourself and have fun.

6. Changing Habits:
Practical Applications of Inner-Game Learning

The previous chapter may have given you some ideas about changes you would like to make in your tennis strokes. The aim of this chapter is to summarize the Inner Game method of how to effect such changes so that they become a spontaneous part of your behavior. Tips are a dime a dozen, and there are good ones and bad ones. But what is more difficult to come by is a workable way to apply tips, to replace one pattern of behavior with a new one. It is in the process of changing habits that most players experience the greatest difficulty. When one learns *how* to break a habit, it is a relatively simple matter to learn *which* ones to break. Once you learn *how* to learn, you have only to discover *what* is worth learning.

Summarized below is what could be called a new way of learning. Actually, it is not new at all; it is the oldest and most natural way of learning—simply a method of forgetting the unnatural ways of learning which we have accumulated. Why is it so easy for a child to pick up a foreign language? Primarily because he hasn't learned how to interfere with his own natural, untaught learning process. The Inner Game way of learning is a return to this childlike way.

By the word "learning" I do not mean the collection of information, but the realization of something which actually changes one's behavior—either external behavior, such as a tennis stroke, or internal behavior, such as a pattern of thought. We all develop characteristic patterns of acting and thinking, and each such pattern exists because it serves a function. The time for change comes when we realize that the same function could be served in a better way. Take the habit of rolling one's racket over after hitting a forehand. This behavior is an attempt to keep the ball from going out, and it exists to produce the desired result. But when the player realizes that by the proper use of topspin the ball can be kept in the court without the risks of error involved in a roll-over follow-through, then the old habit is ready to be dropped.

It is much more difficult to break a habit when there is no adequate replacement for it. This difficulty often exists when we become moralistic about our tennis game. If a player reads in a book that it is wrong to roll his racket over, but is not offered a better way to keep the ball in the court, it will take a great deal of will power to keep his racket flat when he's worried about the ball flying out of the court. As soon as this player gets into a game, you can be sure that he will revert to the stroke that gave some sense of security that his ball would not sail out.

It is not helpful to condemn our present behavior patterns—in this case our present imperfect strokes—as "bad"; it *is* helpful to see what function these habits are serving, so that if we learn a better way to achieve the same end, we can do so. We never repeat any behavior which isn't serving some function or purpose. It is difficult to become aware of the function of any pattern of behavior while we are in the process of blaming ourselves for having a "bad habit." But when we stop trying to suppress or correct the habit, we can see the function it serves, and then an alternative pattern of behavior, which serves the same function better, emerges quite effortlessly.

The Groove Theory of Habits

One hears a lot of talk about grooving one's strokes in tennis. The theory is a simple one: every time you swing your racket in a certain way, you increase the probabilities that you will swing that way again. In this way patterns, called grooves, build up which have a predisposition to repeat themselves. Golfers use the same term. It is as if the nervous system were like a record disk. Every time an action is performed, a slight impression is made in the microscopic cells of the brain, just as a leaf blowing over a fine-grained beach of sand will leave its faint trace. When the same action is repeated, the groove is made slightly deeper. After many similar actions there is a more recognizable groove into which the needle of behavior seems to fall automatically. Then the behavior can be termed grooved.

Because these patterns are serving a function, the behavior is reinforced or rewarded and tends to continue. The deeper the groove in the nervous system, the harder it seems to be to break the habit. We have all had the experience of deciding that we will not hit a tennis ball a certain way again. For example, it would seem to be a simple matter to keep your eye on the ball once you understand the obvious benefits of doing so. But time and again we take our eye off it. Often, in fact, the harder we try to break a habit, the harder it becomes.

If you watch a player trying to correct the habit of rolling his racket over, he will usually be seen gritting his teeth and exerting all his will power to get out of his old groove. Watch his racket. After it hits the ball it will begin to turn over, following the old pattern; then his muscles will tighten and force it to return to the flat position. You can see in the resulting waver exactly where the old habit was halted and the new will power took over. Usually the battle is won only after a great deal of struggle and frustration over the course of some time.

It is a painful process to fight one's way out of a deep mental groove. It's like digging yourself out of a trench. But there is a natural and more childlike method. A child doesn't dig his way out of his old grooves; he simply starts new ones! The groove may be there, but you're not in it unless you put yourself there. If you think you are controlled by a bad habit, then you will feel you have to try to break it. A child doesn't have to break the habit of crawling, because he doesn't think he has a habit. He simply leaves it as he finds walking an easier way to get around.

Habits are statements about the past, and the past is gone. I'm not even sure it exists, since I don't experience it except as a memory or as a concept in the present. There may be a deep groove in the nervous system which will take your forehand on the roll-over trip if you choose to step into that trench; on the other hand, your muscles are as capable as they ever were of swinging your racket through flat. There is no need to strain all the muscles in the arm to keep the racket flat; in fact, it requires fewer muscles to keep it flat than it does to roll it over. Fighting the fantasy of old habits is what causes the conscientious tennis player to strain and tighten unnecessarily.

In short, there is no need to fight old habits. Start new ones. It is the resisting of an old habit that puts you in that trench. Starting a new pattern is easy when done with childlike disregard for imagined difficulties. You can prove this to yourself by your own experience.

Here is a simple summary of the traditional way we have been taught to learn, contrasted with the Inner Game of learning. Experiment with this method and you will discover a workable way to make any desired change in your game.

Making a Change in Stroke, Step by Step

Step 1: Observation

Where do you want to start? What part of your game needs attention? It is not always the stroke that you judge as worst which is the most ready for change. It is good to pick the stroke you most *want* to change. Let the stroke tell you if it wants to change. When you want to change what is ready to change, then the process flows.

For example, let's assume it is your serve that you decide to focus your attention on. The first step is to forget all the ideas you may have in your mind about what is wrong with it as it is. Erase all your previous ideas and begin serving without exercising any conscious control over your stroke. Observe your serve freshly, as it is *now*. Let it fall into its own groove for better or worse. Begin to be interested in it and experience it as fully as you can. Notice how you stand and distribute your weight before beginning your motion. Check your grip and the initial position of your racket. Remember, make no corrections; simply observe without interfering.

Next, get in touch with the rhythm of your serving motion. Feel the path of your racket as it describes its swing. Then serve several balls and watch only your wrist motion. Is your wrist limber or tight? Does it have a full snap or something less? Merely watch. Also observe your toss during several serves. Experience your tossing motion. Does the ball go to the same spot each time? Where is that spot? Finally, become aware of your follow-through. Before long you will feel that you know your serve very well as it is presently grooved. You may also be aware of the results of your motion— that is, the number of balls hit into the net, the speed and accuracy of those that reach the far court. Awareness of what *is,* without judgment, is relaxing, and is the best precondition for change.

It is not unlikely that during this observation period some changes have already begun to take place unintentionally. If so, let the process continue. There's nothing wrong with making unconscious changes; you avoid the complication of thinking that *you* made the change, and thus of the need to remind yourself how to do it.

After you have watched and felt your serve for five minutes or so, you may have a strong idea about the particular element of the stroke that needs attention. Ask your serve how it would like to be different. Maybe it wants a more fluid rhythm; maybe it wants more power, or a greater amount of spin. If 90 percent of the balls are going into the net, it's probably quite obvious what needs to change. In any case, let yourself feel the change most desired, then observe a few more serves.

Step 2: Programming

Let's assume that what is desired in your serve is more power. The next step is to program yourself for more power. One way to do this might be to watch the motion of someone who gets a lot of power in his serve. Don't overanalyze; simply absorb what you see and try to feel what he feels. Listen to the sound of the ball after it hits the racket and watch the results. Then take some time to imagine yourself hitting the ball with power, using the stroke which is natural to you. In your mind's eye, picture yourself serving, filling in as much visual and tactile detail as you can. Hear the sound at impact and see the ball speed toward the service court. Hold this mental image for a minute or so, then ask your body to do whatever is necessary to produce the desired power.

Step 3: Let It Happen

Begin serving again, but with no conscious effort to control your stroke. In particular, resist any temptation to try to hit the ball harder. Simply let your serve begin to serve itself. Having asked for more power, just let it happen. See if your body has figured out how to produce what you want. This isn't magic, so give your body a chance to explore the possibilities. But no matter what the results, keep Self 1 out of it. If increased power does not come immediately, don't force it. Trust the process, and let it happen.

If after a short while the serve does not seem to be moving in the direction of increased power, you may want to return to Step 1. Ask yourself what is inhibiting speed. If you don't come up with an answer, you might ask a pro to take a look. Let's say the pro observes that you are not getting a maximum wrist snap at the top of your swing. He may observe that one reason is that you are holding your racket too tightly to allow for flexibility. The habit of holding the racket tightly and swinging with a stiff wrist usually comes from a conscious attempt to hit the ball hard.

So now you are ready for reprogramming. Let your hand experience what it feels like to hold your racket with medium firmness. Show your wrist what it feels like to move in a full, flexible arc. Don't assume you know just because you've been shown; let yourself *feel* the wrist motion intimately. If you are in any doubt, ask the pro to show you the motion, not tell you about it. Then, in your mind's eye imagine your serving motion, this time seeing distinctly your wrist moving from a fully cocked position, reaching up to the sky, then snapping down until it points to the court on the follow-through. After you have fixed the image of your new wrist motion, serve again. Remember that if you *try* to snap your wrist, it will probably tighten, so just let it go. Let it be flexible; allow it to snap in an ever-increasing arc as much as it wants to. Encourage it, but don't force it. Not trying does not mean being limp. Discover for yourself what it *does* mean.

81

The Usual Way of Learning

Step 1
Criticize or Judge Past Behavior

Examples: I'm hitting my forehand rotten again today . . . Dammit, why do I keep missing those easy setups . . . I'm not doing anything the coach told me to do in my last lesson. You were great rallying, now you're playing worse than your grandmother . . . $%#¢*#¢$!

(The above is usually delivered in a punitive, belittling tone.)

Step 2
Tell Yourself to Change, Instructing with Word Commands Repeatedly

Examples: Keep your racket low, keep your racket low, keep your racket low. Hit the ball in front of you, in front, in front . . . No, dammit, further! Don't flick your wrist, keep it stiff . . . You stupid bum, you did it again . . . Toss the ball good and high this time, then reach up, remember to snap your wrist, and don't change grips in midserve. Hit this one into the crosscourt corner. I'll try harder next time!

Step 3
Try Hard; Make Yourself Do It Right

In this step, Self 1, the ego-mind, having told Self 2 what to do, tries to control the action. Unnecessary body and facial muscles are used. There is a tightness which prevents maximum fluidity of stroke and precision of movement. Self 2 is not trusted.

Step 4
Critical Judgment about Results Leading to Repetition of Process

When one has tried hard to perform an action "right," it is difficult not to become either frustrated at failure or excited by success. Both these emotions are distracting to one's concentration, and prevent full experiencing of what happens. Negative judgment of the results of one's efforts tends to make one *try* even harder; positive evaluation tends to make one *try* to force oneself into the same pattern on the next shot. Both positive and negative thinking inhibit spontaneity.

The Inner Game Way of Learning

Step 1
Observe, Nonjudgmentally, Existing Behavior

Examples: The last three of my backhands landed long, by about two feet. My racket seems to be hesitating, instead of following through all the way. Maybe I should observe the level of my backswing . . . Yes, I thought so, it's well above my waist . . . There, that shot got hit with more pace, yet it stayed in.
(The above is delivered in an interested, somewhat detached tone.)

Step 2
Ask Yourself to Change, Programming with Image and Feel

No commands are used. Self 2 is asked to perform in the desired way to achieve the desired results. Self 2 is shown by use of visual image and felt action any element of stroke desired. If you wish the ball to go to the crosscourt corner, you simply imagine the necessary path of the ball to the target, and feed it into the computer as a problem to be solved. Do not try to correct for errors.

Step 3
Let it Happen!

Having requested your body to perform a certain action, give it the freedom to do it. The body is trusted, without the conscious control of mind. The serve seems to serve itself. *Effort* is initiated by Self 2, but there is no trying by Self 1. Letting it happen doesn't mean going limp; it means letting Self 2 use only the muscles necessary for the job. Nothing is forced; you flow as surely and powerfully as a river.

Step 4
Nonjudgmental, Calm Observation of the Results
Leading to Continuing Observation of Process
until Behavior Is in Automatic

Though the player knows his goal, he is not emotionally involved in achieving it and is therefore able to watch the results calmly and experience the process. By so doing, concentration is best achieved, as is learning at its highest rate of speed; reprogramming is only necessary when results do not conform to the image given. Otherwise only continuing observation of the behavior undergoing change is necessary. Watch it change; don't do the changing.

Step 4: Observation

As you are letting your serve serve itself, your job is simply to observe. Watch the process without exercising control over it. If you feel you want to help, don't. But don't watch with detached objectivity; watch with faith. Actively trust your body to respond to your programming. The more you can bring yourself to put trust in the natural process that is at work, the less you will tend to fall into the usual interfering patterns of trying hard, judging and thinking—and the frustration that inevitably follows.

During this process it is still important to have a certain lack of concern for where the ball is going. As you allow one element of a stroke to change, others will be affected. As you increase your wrist snap, you will alter your rhythm and timing. Initially this may result in inconsistency, but if you continue with the process, simply allowing the serve to serve itself while you remain attentive and patient, the other elements of the serve will make the needed adjustments.

Since power is a function of more than the wrist, after your snap is automatic you may want to let your attention shift to your toss, your balance or some other element. Observe these, program if necessary, and let it happen. Serve until you have reason to believe that a groove has been established. To test if the groove is there, serve a few balls with all your attention solely on the ball. Be engrossed in the seams of the ball as you throw the ball into the air so that you are sure that your mind is not telling your body what to do. If the serve is serving itself in the new manner, a groove has automatically been started.

The process is an incredibly simple one. The important thing is to experience it. Don't intellectualize it. See what it feels like to ask yourself to do something and let it happen without any conscious trying. For most people it is a surprising experience, and the results speak for themselves.

This method of learning can be practiced in most endeavors on or off the court. The more you let yourself perform free of control on the tennis court, the more confidence you tend to gain in the beautiful mechanism that is the human body. The more you trust it, the more capable it seems to become.

But there is one pitfall I should mention. I have noticed that after being thrilled by the improvements they are able to make in their tennis game by letting it happen, students often revert the next day to trying as hard as usual. What is surprising is that though they are playing much worse tennis, they don't seem to mind. At first this puzzled me. Why would one go back to letting Self 1 control the show if the results were so clearly less effective? I had to search myself for the answer. I realized that there was a distinctly different kind of satisfaction gained in the two methods of hitting the ball. When you try hard to hit the ball correctly, and it goes well, you get a certain kind of ego satisfaction. You feel that *you* are in control, that you are master of the situation. But when you simply allow the serve to serve itself, it doesn't seem as if you deserve the credit. It doesn't feel as if it were you who hit the ball. You tend to feel good about the ability of your body, and possibly even amazed by the results, but the credit and sense of personal accomplishment are replaced by another kind of satisfaction. If a person is out on the court mainly to satisfy the desires and doubts of ego, it is likely that in spite of the lesser results, he will choose to let Self 1 play the major role.

When a player experiences what it means to "let go" and allows Self 2 to play the game, not only do his shots tend to gain accuracy and power, but he feels an exhilarating sense of relaxation even during rapid movements. In an attempt to repeat this quality of performance, the player often allows Self 1 to creep back on the scene with a remark such as, "Now I've got the secret to this game; all I have to do is make myself relax." But of course the instant I *try* to make myself relax, true relaxation vanishes, and in its place is a strange phenomenon called "trying to relax." Relaxation happens only when *allowed,* never as a result of "trying" or "making."

Self 1 should not be expected to give up its control all at once; it begins to find its proper role only as one progresses in the art of relaxed concentration.

7. Concentration

Up to this point we have been discussing the art of surrendering Self 1's control and letting the body, Self 2, play the game spontaneously. The primary emphasis has been on giving practical examples of the value of letting go of judging, thinking too much, and trying too hard. But even if the reader is wholly convinced of the value of thus stilling the mind, he may find it difficult to blot out entirely these thinking processes. The quiet mind cannot be achieved by means of intellectual understanding. Only by the *experience* of peace in a moment when the mind is relatively still is one sufficiently encouraged to let go more completely the next time. Very gradually one begins to trust the natural processes which occur when the mind is less and less active.

Even when one has experienced the practical benefits of a still mind, he usually finds it a strangely elusive state. In spite of the fact that I deliver my most effective performance when I permit Self 2 to be the only player of the game, there is still a recurring impulse to think and to want to control my actions. I begin to theorize about how I can achieve the same good results again. I begin to want to regain command. At such moments I recognize this impulse as the seemingly indomitable ego wanting credit, wishing to be something it isn't, and in the process spawning an endless flow of distracting thoughts.

Recently I found myself able to let go of almost all conscious effort on my serve and as a result the serve just seemed to serve itself with rare consistency and power. For a period of about two weeks 90 percent of my first serves went in; I didn't serve a single double fault. Then one day my roommate, another professional, challenged me to a match. I accepted, saying half jokingly, "But you better watch out, I've found the secret to the serve." The next day we played and I served two double faults the first game! The moment I *tried* to apply some "secret," Self 1 was back in the picture again, this time under the subtle guise of "trying to let go." Self 1 wanted to show off to my roommate; it wanted the credit. Even though I soon realized what had happened, the magic of the spontaneous, effortless serving didn't return in its same pure form.

In short, the problem of letting go of Self 1 and its interfering activities is not easy. A clear understanding of the problem can help, but practical demonstrations help more and practicing the process of letting go helps still more. Nevertheless, I do not believe that ultimately the mind can be controlled by the mere act of letting go—that is, by a simply passive process. To still the mind one must learn to put it somewhere. It cannot just be let go; it must be "parked." If peak performance is a function of a still mind, then we are led to the question of where and how to park it. If we achieve this, we have attained concentration.

Concentration is the act of focusing one's attention. As the mind is allowed to focus on a single object, it stills. As the mind is kept in the present, it becomes calm. Concentration means keeping the mind *now* and *here*. Concentration is the supreme art because no art can be achieved without it, while with it, anything can be achieved. One cannot reach the limit of his ability in tennis without learning it; what is even more compelling is that tennis can be a marvelous medium through which skill in concentration can be developed. By learning to concentrate while playing tennis, one develops a skill that can heighten his performance in every other aspect of his life.

All that is needed to begin practicing concentration is an appropriate object on which to focus your attention. In tennis the most convenient and practical object is the ball itself. Probably the most often repeated dictum in tennis is "Watch the ball"; yet few players see it well.

The instruction is an appeal for the player to concentrate. This does not mean to *think* about the ball, to consider how high it is passing over the net or what kind of spin it has; one is simply asked to watch it. Most players look at the ball, or the general area surrounding the ball, but most of the time fall far short of achieving concentration. They look at the ball, but at the same time they are thinking about how they want to hit it, or about what the score will be if they miss it, or about the people talking on the sidelines. The concentrated mind does not admit such distractions, externally or internally; it is totally engrossed in the object of concentration.

Watching the Ball

Watching the ball means to focus your attention on the sight of it. I have found that the most effective way to deepen concentration through sight is to focus on something subtle, not easily perceived. It's easy to see the ball, but not so easy to notice the exact pattern made by its seams as it spins. The practice of watching the seams produces interesting results. After a short time the player discovers that he is seeing the ball much better than when he was just "watching" it. When looking for the pattern made by the seams one naturally watches the ball all the way to one's racket and begins to focus his attention on it earlier than before. The ball should be watched from the time it leaves the opponent's racket to the time it hits yours. (Sometimes the ball even begins to appear bigger or to be moving slower. These are natural results of the concentration of one's conscious energy.)

But seeing the ball better is only a partial benefit of focusing on its seams. Because the pattern made by the spinning ball is so subtle, it tends to engross the mind more completely. The mind is so absorbed in watching the pattern that it forgets to try too hard. To the extent that the mind is preoccupied with the seams, it tends not to interfere with the natural movements of the body. Furthermore, the seams are always here and now, and if the mind is on them it is kept from wandering to the past or future. The practice of this exercise will enable the tennis player to achieve deeper and deeper states of concentration.

Most players who practice seam-watching as a discipline find it helpful almost immediately, but after a while they often discover their minds wandering again. The mind has difficulty focusing on a single object for an extended period of time. Even yogis who practice concentrating on a single external object, such as a rose or a flame, rarely succeed in stilling the mind for long; it simply loses interest and then wanders. Let's face it: as interesting as a tennis ball may be for some, it is not going to easily capture the beelike mind so habituated to flitting from flower to flower. On the other hand, the tennis ball has one quality which makes it a very good object for concentration: it is moving. The mind is attracted by objects in motion; it has been ever since birth.

The question arises: How do you increase your ability to maintain concentration on the ball for long periods of time? On this subject something can be learned from bahkti yoga. Bahkti is the yoga that aims at achieving perfect concentration of mind through devotion. Indian yogis in particular have recognized the power of love in overcoming distraction of mind. Bahkti yoga teaches that love of the object of concentration makes it possible to focus one's attention without wavering, and eventually to become one with that object.

There is a story told by holy men in the East which may make this point more memorable. A seeker after Truth sought out a yoga master and begged him to help him achieve the enlightenment of perfect union with his true self. The Master told him to go into a room and meditate on God for as long as he could. After just two hours the seeker emerged distraught, saying that he could not concentrate, since his mind kept thinking about his much beloved bull he had left at home. The Master then told him to return to the room and meditate on his bull. This time the would-be yogi entered the room and after two days had still not emerged. Finally the Master called for him to come out. From within the seeker replied, "I cannot; my horns are too wide to fit through the door." The seeker had reached such a state of concentration that he had lost all sense of separation from his object of concentration.

As silly as it may sound, one of the most practical ways to increase concentration on the ball is to learn to love it! Get to know the tennis ball; appreciate its qualities. Look at it closely and notice the fine patterns made by the nap. Forget for a moment that it is a tennis ball and look freshly at its shape, its texture, its feel. Consider the inside of the ball and the role played by the empty middle. Allow yourself to know the ball both intellectually and through your senses. Make friends; do anything to start a relationship with it. It will help concentration immeasurably.

Concentration is not staring hard at something. It is not *trying* to concentrate; it is not thinking hard about something. Concentration is fascination of mind. When there is love present, the mind is drawn irresistibly toward the object of love. It is effortless and relaxed, not tense and purposeful. When watching the seams of the ball, allow yourself to fall into relaxed concentration. If your eyes are squinting or straining, you are trying too hard. Let the ball attract your mind, and both it and your muscles will stay relaxed.

The tennis ball should be watched as an object in motion. Watching its seams helps focus your attention on the object itself, but it is just as important to increase your awareness of the *flight* of each ball as it moves toward you, and then again as it leaves your racket. My favorite focus of concentration during a point is on the particular trajectories of each shot, both mine and my opponent's. I notice the height of the ball as it passes over the net, its apparent speed, and with utmost care the angle at which it rises after bouncing. I also observe whether the ball is rising, falling or at its apex in the instant before the racket makes contact. I give the same careful attention to the trajectory of my own shot. Soon I become more and more aware of the rhythm of the alternating shots of each point, and am able to increase my sense of anticipation. It is this rhythm, both seen and heard, which holds facination for my mind and enables it to focus for long periods of time without becoming distracted.

Listening to the Ball

It rarely occurs to a player to listen to the ball, but I have found great value in this form of concentration. When it hits your racket, it makes a distinct sound, the quality of which varies considerably, depending on its proximity to the center of the racket, the angle of the face, the distribution of your weight, and where the ball is met. If you listen closely to the sounds of one ball after another, you will soon be able to distinguish a number of different kinds and qualities of sounds. Soon it is possible to recognize the sound produced by an overspin forehand hit squarely and an underspin forehand hit slightly off center. You will come to know the sound of a flat backhand, and to distinguish it from one hit with an open face.

One day when I was practicing this form of concentration while serving, I began hitting the ball unusually well. I could hear a sharp crack instead of the usual sound at the moment of impact. It sounded terrific, and the ball had more speed and accuracy. After I realized how well I was serving, I resisted the temptation to figure out why, and simply asked my body to do whatever was necessary to reproduce that "crack." I held the sound in my memory, and to my amazement my body reproduced it time and again.

Through this experience I learned how effective the remembering of certain sounds can be as a cue for the built-in computer within our brains. While one listens to the sounds of his forehand, he can hold in his memory the sound that results from solid contact; as a result, the body will tend to repeat the elements of behavior which produced that sound. This technique can be particularly useful in learning the different kinds of serves. There is a distinct difference in the sounds of a flat, slice, and twist serve. Similarly, one can learn to achieve the desired amount of spin in a second serve by listening closely to the sounds of balls hit with varying amounts of spin. Further, listening to the sound of the ball when volleying can improve both volley footwork and racket work. When a volley is met squarely at just the right moment, the action produces a wonderfully memorable sound.

Some players find the sound of the ball more mind-absorbing than watching the seams because it is something they've never done before. Actually there is no reason why both means of concentration cannot be employed on each shot, since one need listen only at the instant of contact.

I have found that the practice of listening to the ball is best used during practice. If you become sensitive to sound in practice, you will find that you will then use sound automatically during a match to encourage the repetition of solid shots. The habit will increase the number of balls hit in the center of your racket.

Feeling

When I was twelve years old, I heard my pro say of my doubles partner, "He really knows where his racket head is." I didn't know what he meant, but I intuited its importance and never forgot the remark. Few players understand the importance of concentrating attention on the feel of the racket as they are holding it. There are two things that a player *must* know on every shot: where the ball is and where his racket is. If he loses contact with either of these he is in trouble. Most players have learned to put visual attention on the ball, but many have only the vaguest notion about where their racket head is most of the time. The critical time to know the position of the racket is when it is behind you, and this requires concentration through the sense of feel.

On the forehand your hand is about eighteen inches from the center of your racket. This means that even a tiny change in the angle of your wrist can produce a significant difference in the position of the center of the racket. Similarly, the slightest change in the angle of the face of the racket can have a substantial effect on the trajectory of the ball. Hence, to achieve consistency and accuracy, you must become extraordinarily sensitive to feel.

It would be useful for all tennis players to undergo some "sensitivity training" with their bodies. The easiest way to get such training is simply to focus your attention on your body during practice. Ideally, someone should throw balls to you, or hit them so that they bounce in approximately the same spot each time. Then, paying relatively little attention to the ball, you can experience what it feels like to hit balls the way you hit them. You should spend some time merely feeling the exact path of your racket on your backswing. The greatest attention should be placed on the feel of your arm and hand at the moment just before they swing forward to meet the ball. Also become sensitive to how the handle feels in your hand. Are you squeezing too hard?

There are many ways to increase one's awareness of muscle feel. One is to take each of your strokes in slow motion. Each can be performed as an exercise, in which all attention is placed on the feel of the moving parts of the body. Get to know the feel of every inch of your stroke, every muscle in your body. Then when you increase your stroke speed to normal and begin hitting, you may be particularly aware of certain muscles. For instance, when I hit my best backhands, I am aware that my shoulder muscle, rather than my forearm, is pulling my arm through. By remembering the feel of that muscle before hitting a backhand, I program myself to attain the full benefit of the power it generates. Similarly, on my forehand I am particularly aware of my triceps when my racket is below the ball. By becoming sensitive to the feel of that muscle, I decrease my tendency to take my racket back too high.

It is also important to become more aware of rhythm. You can greatly improve your power and timing merely by paying attention during practice to the rhythm with which you hit each of your strokes. Every player has a rhythm natural to himself. If you learn to concentrate on the sense of rhythm, it is not difficult to fall into the rhythm most natural and effective for you. Rhythm can never be achieved by being overly purposeful about it; you have to let it happen. But sensitivity to rhythm developed through concentration helps. Those who have practiced concentrating on the feel of the path of their racket usually find that without intentional effort their stroke begins to slow down and to simplify. Both the rapid jerks and the fancy stuff tend to disappear and consistency and power to increase.

Just as it is helpful to become more aware of the sound of the ball, it is also useful to practice focusing on the feel of the ball at impact. You can notice subtle and not so subtle differences in the vibration sent up your hand when the ball strikes the racket, depending on where contact is made, your distribution of weight, and the angle of the face of your racket. Again, you can program the best results by remembering as precisely as possible the feel in your hand, wrist and arm after a good solid hit. Practicing this kind of feel develops what is called "touch," and is particularly beneficial in hitting drop shots and lobs.

In short, become aware of your body. Know what it feels like to move your body into position, as well as how it feels to swing your racket. Remember: it is almost impossible to feel or see anything well if you are *thinking* about how you should be moving. Forget should's and experience *is*. In tennis there are only one or two elements to be aware of visually, but there are many things to feel. Expanding sensory knowledge of your body will greatly speed the process of developing skill.

In the last 6 pages, I have discussed ways of sharpening three of the five senses and expanding the awareness which is received through them. Practice them not as a list of tennis do's and don't's, but one at a time at your own rhythm.

(To complete the cycle, I should say something about taste and smell, but as far as I know, these senses have little or nothing to do with one's ability to play good tennis. Perhaps I've missed something. The best I can do is to pass on the advice of my coach at Harvard, Jack Barnaby, who used to tell us to attack the volley by keeping our faces near the ball. "Bite the ball!" he used to shout. It's good advice, for it helps you to hit the ball in front of you and aids in balance.)

The Theory of Concentration

The practices mentioned above can speed learning to play your best tennis. But we have come to an important point that should not be passed over quickly. After I developed by practice some small ability to concentrate my mind, I discovered that concentration was not only a means to an end, but something of tremendous value in itself. As a result, instead of using concentration to help my tennis, I now use tennis as a means to further increase concentration. For those interested, I will elaborate this point.

Whatever we experience on a tennis court is known to us by virtue of awareness—that is, by the consciousness within us. It is consciousness which makes possible awareness of the sights, sounds, feelings and thoughts which compose what we call "experience." It is self-evident that one cannot experience anything *outside* of consciousness. Consciousness is that which makes all things and events knowable. Without consciousness eyes could not see, ears could not hear, and mind could not think. Consciousness is like a pure light energy whose power is to make events knowable, just as an electric light makes objects visible. Consciousness could be called the light of lights because it is by its light that all other lights become visible.

In the human body the light energy of consciousness does its knowing through several limited facilities—namely, the five senses and the intellect. Through eyes, it knows sights; through ears, sounds; and through mind it knows concepts, facts and ideas. All that ever happens to us, all that we ever do, is known to us through the light energy of this awareness.

Right now your consciousness is aware through your eyes of the words in this sentence. But other things are also happening within the range of your consciousness. If you stop to listen closely to whatever your ears can hear, you will no doubt be able to hear sounds which you previously weren't aware of, even though they were going on while you were reading. If you now listen to these sounds closely, you will hear them better—that is, you will be able to know them better. Probably you were not aware of how your tongue feels in your mouth—but in all likelihood after reading the foregoing words, you now are. While you were reading or listening to the sights and sounds around you, you were not aware of the feeling of your tongue, but with the slightest suggestion, the mind directs the focus of attention from one thing to another. When attention is allowed to rest in one place, it comes to know that place because attention is focused consciousness, and consciousness is that power of knowing.

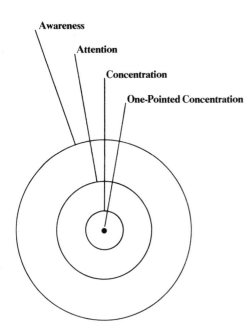

Awareness

Attention

Concentration

One-Pointed Concentration

Concentration, then, is a further focusing of conscious energy. Consider this analogy. Consciousness is similar to an electric lamp shining in a dark forest. Let's say that this lamp has the power of 1000 watts. By virtue of this light it is possible to see and know the forest within a certain radius. The closer an object is to the light, the more it will be illuminated and the greater the detail that will be visible. Objects farther away can be seen only vaguely. But if we put a reflector around one side of the lamp, preventing the light from shining there, all the light energy will be available to illuminate what is in front of it. Those objects that were seen previously will now appear with much greater clarity, while those that were previously invisible will now be knowable. This is the power of attention, or the focusing of conscious energy. Concentration is analogous to focusing all 1000 watts through an ever-decreasing aperture. When all 1000 watts are focused through one point, the light will have the maximum power. Whatever one chooses to learn can be known with the benefit of total illumination. No shadows, no secrets; all is revealed.

There is much talk these days about higher consciousness. What is higher consciousness but seeking more of what is already there? As one's ability to focus the light energy of consciousness increases, the effective range of his vision increases. He seems to see things that are invisible, such as the thoughts of others, the so-called past or the future. Actually, he is only seeing what is already there and is now visible to him because he can focus the energy of his awareness.

The value of concentration becomes clear as we grow to understand that nothing can be enjoyed or appreciated if it cannot be known. Beauty cannot be enjoyed unless one can know it. Peace cannot be enjoyed unless it can be known. The same goes for love and truth—in fact, anything that is valued by man. By increasing the effective power of awareness, concentration allows us to throw more light on whatever we value knowing, and to that extent enables us to know and enjoy it more.

The Here and Now of the Tennis Court

Back to the tennis court. When one concentrates on the court, he focuses his awareness in two dimensions, the *here* and the *now*—that is, in space and in time. The first part of this chapter suggested several "here"s as objects of concentration. The seams focus awareness more exactly in space than merely the ball itself does, and as you add awareness of one element of the game of tennis after another—from the sound of the ball to the feel of each part of each stroke—greater knowledge is gained.

But it is also necessary to learn to focus awareness in the *now*. This simply means tuning into what is happening in the present. The greatest lapses in concentration come when we allow our minds to project what is about to happen or to dwell on what has already happened. How easily the mind absorbs itself in the world of "what if"s. "What if I lose this point?" it thinks; "then I'll be behind 5–3 on his serve. If I don't break his serve, then I'll have lost the first set and probably the match. I wonder what Martha will say when she hears I lost to George." At this point it is not uncommon for the mind to lapse into a little fantasy about Martha's reaction to hearing the news that you have lost to George. Meanwhile, back in the now, the score is still 3–4, 30–40, and you are barely aware that you are on the court; the conscious energy you need to perform at your peak in the now has been leaking into an imagined future.

Similarly, the mind often draws one's attention into the past. "If the linesman hadn't called that last serve out, the score would be deuce and I wouldn't be in this mess. The same thing happened to me last week, and it cost me the match. It made me lose my concentration, then confidence, and now the same thing is happening again. I wonder why. One nice aspect of tennis is that before long you or your opponent is going to hit a ball, and this will summon you back to the present. But usually part of our energy is left in the thought world of past or future, so that the present is not seen with all of one's light awareness. As a result, objects look dim, the ball seems to come faster, appears smaller, and even the court seems to shrink.

Since the mind seems to have a will of its own, how can one learn to keep it in the present? By practice. There is no other way. Every time your mind starts to leak away, simply bring it gently back. Also practice being more and more present. This can be developed especially well with the volley and return of serve. I use a ball machine with a wide range in velocity, and have a simple drill which helps players experience what it means to be more in the present. I ask students to stand at net in the volley position, and then set the machine to shoot balls at three-quarter speed. From being initially casual, they suddenly become more alert. At first the balls seem too fast for them, but soon their responses quicken. Gradually I turn the machine to faster and faster speeds, and the volleyers become more concentrated. When they are responding quickly enough to hit the top-speed balls and believe they are at the peak of their concentration, I move the machine to midcourt, fifteen feet closer than before. At this point students will often lose some concentration as a degree of fear intrudes. Their forearms tense slightly, making their movements less quick and accurate. "Relax your forearm. Relax your mind. Simply relax into the present, focus on the seams of the ball, and let it happen." Soon they are again able to meet the ball in front of them with the center of their rackets. There is no smile of self-satisfaction, merely total absorption in each moment. Afterward some players say that the ball seemed to slow down; others remark how weird it is to hit balls when you don't have time to think about it. All who enter even a little into that state of being present will experience a calmness and a degree of ecstasy which they will want to repeat.

The practical consequences to your volley of increasing your alertness are obvious. Most volleys are missed either because contact is made too far behind the player, or because they are not hit on the center of the racket. Becoming more aware of the present makes it easier to know where the ball is at all times and to react soon enough to meet it at the instant of your choice. Some people think that they are just too slow to return a hard drive when they are at net. But time is a relative thing, and it really *is* possible to slow it down. Consider: there are 1000 milliseconds in every second. That's a lot of milliseconds. Alertness is a measure of how many nows you are aware of in a given period, and everyone's alertness can be heightened with the practice of concentration. The result is simple: you become more aware of what is going on as you learn to keep your attention in the now.

I have found that the most direct means of increasing one's ability to concentrate is through the practice of meditation. After practicing a certain technique of meditation for several months, I was surprised to find my alertness so increased that I could completely alter the style and tactic of my return of serve. Instead of standing behind the base line to receive a hard serve, I found it possible to receive serve standing only one foot behind the service line! Even against hard first serves I seemed to have the time needed to respond and pick up the ball just a split second after it bounced. There was no time for a backswing and no time to think about what I was doing. There would just be a calm concentration followed by a quick movement to meet the ball—initiated even before the ball had passed over the net—a follow-through which gave direction and depth to the ball, and then in the next instant I would be at net—well before the server! The server, seeing me standing at the service line to receive his serve, would have to deal mentally with what he might take to be an insult to his serve; he would often double-fault more than once in an effort to teach me a lesson. His next problem would be hitting a volley passing shot from somewhere within no man's land.

The reader might quite naturally think that this tactic would be impossible against a really first-rate serve. Not true. After only a few months of experimenting with this return of serve, I found it possible to use it to great advantage in tournament play. The more I used it, the quicker and more accurate my reactions became. Concentration seemed to slow time down, giving me the necessary awareness to see and place the ball. The fact that I met the ball on the rise cut off all the angle that a server usually gets on his serve after it bounces. And the fact that I could reach the net before the server gave me control of the commanding position on the court. I believe that if some top-flight amateur or pro practiced enough to perfect this technique he could start a minor revolution in the game of tennis; he could reverse the longstanding advantage of the server.

Concentration during a Match

Most of the ways for developing concentration mentioned earlier are best employed during practice. In a match it is usually best to pick one object of concentration—whatever works best for you—and stick with it. For example, if the seams of the ball tend to keep you centered in the here and now, there is no need to focus on sound or feel. Often the fact that you are playing a match will help you to concentrate. During the course of a point, you often find yourself in a state of relatively deep concentration in which you are only aware of what is happening at that instant. The critical time is between points! After the last shot of a rally, the mind leaves its focus on the ball and is free to wander. It is at this moment that thoughts about the score, your erratic backhand, business, the children, dinner and so forth tend to siphon your energy away from the here and now. Then it is difficult to regain the same level of concentration before the next point begins.

How to stay concentrated in the here and now between points? My own device, and one that has been effective for many of my students, is to focus attention on breathing. Some object or activity which is always present is needed. What is more here and now than one's breathing? Putting attention on breathing simply means observing my breath going in, going out, going in, going out in its natural rhythm. It does *not* mean intentionally controlling my breath.

Breathing is a remarkable phenomenon. Whether we intend to or not, we breathe. Awake or asleep, it is always happening. Even if we try to stop, some force will soon overpower our efforts and we will take a breath. Thus, when we focus attention on breathing we are putting our conscious energy on something closely connected to the life energy of the body. Also, breathing is a very basic rhythm. It is said that in breathing man recapitulates the rhythm of the universe. When the mind is fastened to the rhythm of breathing, it tends to become absorbed and calm. Whether on or off the court, I know of no better way to begin to deal with anxiety than to place the mind on one's breathing process. Anxiety is fear about what may happen in the future, and it occurs only when the mind is imagining what the future may bring. But when your attention is on the here and now, the actions which need to be done in the present have their best chance of being successfully accomplished, and as a result the future will become the best possible present.

So after a point has ended and I'm returning to position or going to pick up a ball, I place my mind on my breathing. The second my mind starts wondering about whether I'm going to win or lose the match, I bring it gently back to my breath and relax in its natural and basic motion. In this way, by the time the next point is ready to start, I am able to be even more concentrated than I was in the midst of the previous one. This technique is not only useful for me in stopping the mind from fretting about bad shots, but keeps me from being self-conscious about unusually good shots.

If you have never done so, you might experiment with this exercise right now. Simply focus on your breath, absorbing more and more conscious energy into the awareness of the experience of breathing. It may help to allow your hands to open as you inhale and to close as you exhale. Then ask your hands to open and close slightly less. Don't force your fingers to do this; simply ask them and let them respond. If your mind begins to wander, bring it back gently to your breathing. As your mind stills and settles into a calm state, let yourself be alert to every split second of breathing and experience as fully as you can this state of relative quiet. When this same calm alertness is maintained on the tennis court, you are ready to perform nearer the limit of your ability. When I am waiting near the service line, about to receive a powerful serve, I absorb my mind as deeply as it will go into my breath; in this way I have found I can reach my peak of alertness while remaining calm.

Breath and Strokes

Just as the breath has a twofold rhythm which echoes the ebb and flow of the tides, the rising and setting of the sun, the up and the down, the in and out, the potential and the actual, the masculine and the feminine, so too do most of the strokes in tennis repeat this rhythm. Ground strokes have a back and a forth, a feminine and a masculine component. Without a backswing there is no follow-through. Without a follow-through, the backswing is of no use.

There is a practical application of this notion. One way to achieve a natural rhythm in your ground strokes is to allow your swing to coincide with your breathing. Inhale with your backswing and exhale with your follow-through. Match your stroke with your breathing, not your breathing with your strokes. You will find that in a short period any jerkiness and irregularity of rhythm will begin to fall away. I don't recommend this practice during a match, for the obvious reason that it is difficult to regulate your breath to the irregularities of the point, but if you practice matching stroke with breath in practice, the basic rhythm will become a part of your game. The same idea is effective with your serve. Inhale as you toss the ball up and take your racket back; this tends to cause you to rise and meet the ball at the top of your swing. Then exhale or hold your breath at the moment you swing to meet the ball.

Lapses in Concentration Occur

It is perplexing to wonder why we ever leave the here and now. Here and now are the only place and time when one ever enjoys himself or accomplishes anything. Most of our suffering takes place when we allow our minds to imagine the future or mull over the past. Nonetheless, few people are ever satisfied with what is before them at the moment. Our desire that things be different from what they are pulls our minds into an unreal world, and in consequence we are less able to appreciate what the present has to offer. Our minds have the reality of the present only when we prefer the unreality of the past or future. To begin to understand my own lapses of concentration I had to know what I was really desiring, and it soon became clear to me that there were more desires operating in me on the court than simply to play tennis. In other words, tennis was not the only game I was playing on the court. Part of the process of attaining a concentrated state of mind is to know and resolve these conflicting desires; the following chapter attempts to shed light on this process.

8. Games People Play on the Court

That something else besides tennis is being played on the courts is obvious to the most casual observer. Regardless of whether he is watching the game at a country club, a public park or a private court, he will see players suffering everything from minor frustration to major exasperation. He will see the stomping of feet, shaking of fists, war dances, rituals, pleas, oaths and prayers; rackets are thrown against fences in anger, into the air for joy, or pounded against the concrete in disgust. Balls that are in will be called out, and vice versa. Linesmen are threatened, ball boys scolded and the integrity of friends questioned. On the faces of players you may observe, in quick succession, shame, pride, ecstasy and despair. Smug complacency gives way to high anxiety, cockiness to hang-dog disappointment. Anger and aggression of varying intensity are expressed both openly and in disguised forms. If an observer was watching the game for the first time, it would be hard for him to believe that all this drama could be contained on a mere tennis court, between love-all and game, set and match.

There is no end to the variety of attitudes toward the game. Not only can the full spectrum of emotional response be observed on the court, but also a wide range in the motivations of its players. Some care only about winning. Some are amazingly tenacious about warding off defeat, but can't win a match point if it's offered to them. Many don't care how they play, just as long as they look good, and some simply don't care at all. Some cheat their opponents; others cheat themselves. Some are always bragging about how good they are; others constantly tell you how poorly they are playing. There are even a small handful who are out on the court simply for fun and exercise.

In his widely read book, *Games People Play,* Eric Berne described the subliminal games that lie beneath the surface of human interaction. He made it remarkably clear that what *appears* to be happening between people is only a small part of the story. The same seems to be true on the tennis court, and since, to play any game well, one must know as much as possible about it, I include here a brief guide to the games people play on the tennis court, followed by a brief account of my own search for a game worth playing. I suggest that this guide be read not as an exercise in self-analysis, but as a key to discovering how to have more fun while playing tennis. It's difficult to have fun or to achieve concentration when your ego is engaged in a life-and-death struggle. Self 2 will never be allowed to express spontaneity and excellence when Self 1 is playing some heavy ulterior game involving its self-image. Yet as one recognizes the games of Self 1, a degree of liberation can be achieved. When it is, you can discriminate objectively and discover for yourself the game you think is really worth playing.

A brief explanation of the meaning of "game." Eric Berne uses the word to mean an interaction between people involving an ulterior motive. In an inspiring book called *The Master Game,* Robert S. De Ropp writes that a game is "essentially a trial of strength or a trial of wits played within a matrix which is defined by rules." Every game involves at least one player, a goal, some obstacle between the player and his goal, a field (physical or mental) on which the game is played, and a motive for playing.

In the guide below I have named three categories of games with their aims and motives for playing. I call these games Good-o, Friends-o and Health-o–Fun-o, and they are played both on and off the courts. Under each of these major categories are subgames, which have subaims and submotivations, and even each subgame has numerous variations. Moreover, most people play hybrid forms of two or three games at a time.

Game 1: Good-o

**General Aim:
To Achieve Excellence**

**General Motive:
To Prove Oneself "Good"**

Subgame A: Perfect-o

Thesis: How good can I get? In Perfect-o, "good" is measured against a standard of performance. In golf, it is measured against par; in tennis, against self-conceived expectations or those of parents, coach or friends.

Aim: Perfection; to reach the highest standard possible.

Motive: The desire to prove oneself competent and worthy of the respect of self and others.

Obstacles:

External: The never-closing gap between one's idea of perfection and one's apparent abilities.

Internal: Self-criticism for not being as close to perfection as one would like, leading to discouragement, compulsively trying too hard and a sense of inferiority; fear of not measuring up.

Subgame B: Compete-o

Thesis: I'm better than you. Here, "good" is measured against the performance of other players rather than against a set standard. Maxim: It's not how well I play, but whether I win or lose that counts.

Aim: To be the best; to win; to defeat all comers.

Motive: Desire to be at the top of the heap. Stems from need for admiration and control.

Obstacles:
External: There is always someone around who can beat you; the rising ability of the young.
Internal: The mind's preoccupation with comparing oneself with others, thus preventing spontaneous action; thoughts of inferiority alternating with superiority, depending on the competition; fear of defeat.

Subgame C: Image-o
Thesis: Look at me! "Good" is measured by appearance. Neither winning nor true competence is as important as style.
Aim: To look good, flashy, strong, brilliant, smooth, graceful.
Motive: Desire for attention, praise.
Obstacles:
External: One can never look good enough. What looks good to one person does not look so good to another.
Internal: Confusion about who one really is. Fear of not pleasing everyone and of imagined loneliness.

Main Game 2: Friends-o

General Aim: To Make or Keep Friends

General Motive: Desire for Friendship

Subgame A: Status-o
Thesis: We play at the country club. It's not so important how good you are as where you play and who plays with you.
Aim: To maintain or improve social status.
Motive: Desire for the friendship of the prominent.
Obstacles:
External: The cost of keeping up with the Joneses.
Internal: Fear of losing one's social position.

Subgame B: Togetherness-o
Thesis: All my good friends play tennis. You play to be with your friends. To play too well would be a mistake.
Aim: To meet or keep friends.
Motive: Desire for acceptance and friendship.
Obstacles:
External: Finding the time, the place and the friends.
Internal: Fear of ostracism.

Subgame C: Husband-o or Wife-o
Thesis: My husband (or wife) is always playing, so . . . Enough said?
Aim: To see your spouse.
Motive: Loneliness.

Obstacles:
External: Becoming good enough for spouse to play with you.
Internal: Doubts that loneliness can be overcome on the tennis court. (See also internal obstacles of Perfect-o.)

Main Game 3: Health-o-Fun-o

**General Aim:
Mental or Physical
Health or Pleasure**

**General Motive:
Health and/or Fun**

Subgame A: Health-o
Thesis: Played on doctor's advice, or as part of self-initiated physical improvement or beautification program.
Aim: Exercise, work up a sweat, relax the mind.
Motive: Health, vitality, desire for prolongation of youth.
Obstacles:
External: Finding someone of like motive to play with.
Internal: Doubts that tennis is really helping. The temptation to be drawn into Perfect-o or Good-o.

Subgame B: Fun-o
Thesis: Played neither for winning nor to become "good," but for fun alone. (A game rarely played in its pure form.)
Aim: To have as much fun as possible.
Motive: Desire for enjoyment.
Obstacles:
External: Finding someone of like motive to play with.
Internal: Learning to appreciate fully the subtleties of the game. The temptation to be drawn into Good-o or Friends-o.

Subgame C: High-o
Thesis: Played to raise one's awareness. Very rarely played in pure form.
Aim: Higher consciousness.
Motive: Desire to transcend ordinary consciousness.
Obstacles:
External: None.
Internal: The attachments and fluctuations of the ego-mind.

The Competitive Ethic and the Rise of Good-o

Most tennis players in our society, regardless of the reasons which they may think motivated them to take up the sport in the first place, end up playing one or another version of Good-o. Many start tennis as a weekend sport in the hope of getting exercise and a needed relief from the pressures of daily life, but they end by setting impossible standards of excellence for themselves and often become more frustrated and tense on the court than off it.

How can the quality of one's tennis assume such importance that it causes anxiety, anger, depression and self-doubt? The answer seems to be deeply rooted in a basic pattern of our culture. In the New World, excellence is valued in all things. We live in an achievement-oriented society where a man is measured by his competence in various endeavors. Even before we received praise or blame for our first report card, we were loved or ignored for how well we performed our very first actions. From this pattern, one basic message came across loud, clear and often: you are a good person and worthy of respect only if you do things successfully. Of course, the kind of things needed to be done well to deserve love varies from family to family, but the underlying equation between self-worth and performance has been nearly universal.

Now, that's a pretty heavy equation, for it means that to some extent every achievement-oriented action becomes a criterion for defining one's self-worth.

If someone plays bad golf, it comes somehow to mean that he is not quite as worthy of respect, his own or of others, as he would be if he played well. If he is the club champion, he is considered a winner, and thus a more valuable person in our society. It then follows that the intelligent, beautiful and competent tend to regard themselves as *better* people.

When love and respect depend on winning or doing well in a competitive society, it is inevitable (since every winner requires a loser and every top performance many inferior ones) that there will be many people who feel a lack of love and respect. Of course, these people will try hard to win the respect they lack, and the winners will try equally hard not to lose the respect they have won. In this light, it is not difficult to see why playing well has come to mean so much to us.

But who said that I am to be measured by how well I do things? In fact, who said that I should be measured at all? Who indeed? What is required to disengage oneself from this trap is a clear knowledge that the value of a human being cannot be measured by performance—or by any other arbitrary measurement. Like Jonathan L. Seagull, are we not an immeasurable energy in the process of manifesting, by degrees, an unlimited potential? Is this not so of every human and perhaps every life form? If so, it doesn't really make sense to measure ourselves in comparison with other immeasurable beings. In fact, we are what we are; we are *not* how well we happen to perform at a given moment. The grade on a report card may measure an ability in arithmetic, but it doesn't measure the person's value. Similarly, the score of a tennis match may be an indication of how well I performed or how hard I tried, but it does not define my identity, nor give me cause to consider myself as something more or less than I was before the match.

My Search for a Game Worth Playing

At about the age I was tall enough to see over the net, my father started me on tennis. I played the game more or less casually with my cousins and older sister until I was eleven, when I received my first tennis lesson from a new pro named John Gardiner at Pebble Beach, California. That same year, I played in my first tournament in the "under 11" division of the National Hardcourt Championships. The night before the match, I dreamed of the glory of being a dark-horse winner. My first match was a nervous but easy victory. My second, against the second-seeded player, ended in a 6–4, 6–4 defeat and with me sobbing bitterly. I had no idea why winning meant so much to me.

The next few summers I played tennis every day. I would wake myself at 7 A.M., make and eat my own breakfast in five minutes, then run miles to the Pebble Beach courts. I usually arrived a good hour before anyone else and would spend the time hitting fore- hands and backhands tirelessly against a backboard. During the day, I would play ten or fifteen sets, drill and take lessons, not stop- ping until there was no longer enough light to see the ball. Why? I really didn't know. If someone had asked, I would have said that it was because I liked tennis. Though this was partially true, it was pri- marily because I was deeply involved in the game of Perfect-o. There was something I seemed to want badly to prove to myself. Winning was important to me in tournaments, but playing well was important day by day; I wanted to get better and better. My style was to think I would never win, and then to try to surprise myself and others. I was hard to beat, but I had an equally difficult time winning close matches. Though I hated losing, I didn't really enjoy beating someone else; I found it slightly embarrassing. I was a tirelessly hard worker and never stopped trying to improve my strokes.

By the time I was fifteen I had won the National Hardcourt Championship in the boys' division, and felt the rush of excitement at winning a major tournament. Earlier the same summer I went to the National Championships at Kalamazoo and lost in the quarter finals to the seventh-seeded player, 6–3, 0–6, 10–8. In the last set, I had been ahead 5–3, 40–15 on my serve. I was nervous but optimistic. In the first match point, I double-faulted in an attempt to serve an ace on my second serve. In the second, I missed the easiest put-away volley possible in front of a packed grandstand. For many years thereafter, I replayed that match point in countless dreams, and it is as vivid in my memory now as it was on that day twenty years ago. Why? What difference did it really make? It didn't occur to me to ask.

By the time I entered college, I had given up the idea of proving my worth through the vehicle of championship tennis, and was happy to settle for being "a good amateur." I put most of my energy into intellectual endeavors, sometimes grade-grubbing, sometimes a sincere search for Truth. From my sophomore year onward I played varsity tennis, and found that on days when I did poorly in my academic work, I would usually perform badly also on the tennis court. I would try hard to prove on the court what I had difficulty proving scholastically, but would usually find that lack of confidence in the one area tended to infect the other. Fortunately, the reverse was also true. During four years of collegiate play, I was almost always nervous when I walked onto a court to play a match. By the time I was a senior and had been elected captain of the team, I was of the opinion that competition really didn't prove anything. I knew intellectually that being good at tennis wasn't a valid test of manhood—or of anything else of importance—but I was still tight before a match.

After graduation I gave up competitive tennis for ten years and embarked on a career in education. I became interested in learning theory, and in 1970 while teaching tennis during the summer, began to gain some insights into the learning process. Deciding to continue teaching tennis, I developed what came to be called yoga tennis, the precursor to the Inner Game way of learning. It applied to tennis some of the principles I'd learned in yoga, and seemed to increase tremendously the learning rate of students. It also had a beneficial effect on my game. Learning a little about the art of concentration helped my game revive quickly, and soon I was consistently playing better than ever. After I became the club pro at the Meadowbrook Club in Seaside, California, I found that even though I didn't have much time to work on my own strokes, by applying the principles I was teaching I could maintain a game which was seldom defeated by anyone in the local area.

As an instructor of yoga tennis, I didn't concern myself with winning; I simply attempted to achieve and express a high degree of excellence. But one day, after playing particularly well against a very good player, I began wondering how I might fare in tournament competition. I felt confident of my game; still, I hadn't played against ranked players. So I entered a tournament at the Berkeley Tennis Club in which Laver, Rosewall and other top-ranking players were competing. On the appointed weekend, I drove to Berkeley with confidence, but by the time I arrived I had started to question my own ability. Everyone there seemed to be six foot five and to be carrying five or six rackets. I recognized many of the players from tennis magazines, but none of them seemed to recognize me. The atmosphere was very different from that of Meadowbrook, my little pond where I was chief frog. Suddenly I found my previous optimism turning to pessimism. I was doubting my game. Why? Had anything happened to it from the time I left my club three hours before?

My first match was against a player who literally *was* six foot five. Even though he carried only three rackets, as we each walked to a backcourt my knees felt a bit wobbly and my wrist didn't seem as strong as usual. I tested it several times, tightening my hand on the handle of my racket. I wondered what would happen out on the court. But when we began to warm up, I soon saw that my opponent wasn't nearly as good as I had imagined. Had I been giving him a lesson, I knew exactly what I would tell him, and I quickly categorized him as a "better-than-average club player" and felt better.

However, an hour later, with the score 4–1 in his favor in the second set, and having lost the first set 6–3, I began to realize that I was about to be beaten by a "better-than-average club player." All during the match I had been on edge, missing easy shots and playing inconsistently. It seemed my concentration was off just enough so that I missed lines by inches and hit the top of the net with every other volley.

As it worked out, my opponent, on the verge of a clear victory, faltered. I don't know what was happening inside his head, but he couldn't finish me off. He lost the second set 7–5 and the next 6–1, but as I walked off the court, I had no sense that I had won the match—rather, that he had lost it.

I began thinking immediately of my next match against a highly ranked player in northern California. I knew that he was a more experienced tournament player than I and probably more skilled. I certainly didn't want to play the way I had during the first round; it would be a rout. But my knees were still shaky, my mind didn't seem able to focus clearly, and I was nervous. Finally, I sat down in seclusion to see if I could come to grips with myself. I began by asking myself, "What's the worst that can happen?"

The answer was easy: "I could lose 6–0, 6–0."

"Well, what if you did? What then?"

"Well . . . I'd be out of the tournament and go back to Meadow-brook. People would ask me how I did, and I would say that I lost in the second round to So-and-So."

They'd say sympathetically, "Oh, he's pretty tough. What was the score?" Then I would have to confess; love and love.

"What would happen next?" I asked myself.

"Well, word would quickly get around that I had been trounced up at Berkeley, but soon I'd start playing well again and before long life would be back to normal."

I had tried to be as honest as I could about the worst possible results. They weren't good, but neither were they unbearable— certainly not bad enough to get upset about. Then I asked myself, "What's the best that could happen?"

Again the answer was clear: I could win 6–0, 6–0.

"Then what?"

"I'd have to play another match, and then another until I was beaten, which in a tournament like this was soon inevitable. Then I would return to my own club, report how I did, receive a few pats on the back, and soon all would again return to normal."

Staying in the tournament another round or two didn't seem overwhelmingly attractive, so I asked myself a final question: "Then what do you *really* want?"

The answer was quite unexpected. What I really wanted, I realized, was to overcome the nervousness that was preventing me from playing my best. I wanted to overcome the inner obstacle that had plagued me for so much of my life. I wanted to win the *inner* game.

Having come to this realization, knowing what I really wanted, I walked toward my match with a new sense of enthusiasm. In the first game, I double-faulted three times and lost my serve, but from then on I felt a new certainty. It was as if a huge pressure had been relieved, and I was out there playing with all the energies at my command. As it worked out, I was never able to break my opponent's spinning, left-handed serve, but I didn't lose my own serve again until the last game in the second set. I had lost 6–4, 6–4, but I walked off the courts feeling that I had won. I had lost the external game, but had won the game I had wanted to, my *own* game, and I felt very happy. Indeed, when a friend came up to me after the match and asked how I'd done, I was tempted to say, "I won!"

For the first time I recognized the existence of the Inner Game, and its importance to me. I didn't know what the rules of the game were, nor exactly what its aim was, but I did sense that it involved something more than winning a trophy.

9. The Meaning of Competition

In contemporary Western culture there is a great deal of controversy about competition. One segment values it highly, believing that it is responsible for Western progress and prosperity. Another segment says that competition is bad; that it pits one person against another and is therefore divisive; that it leads to enmity between people and therefore to a lack of cooperation and eventual ineffectualness. Those who value competition believe in sports such as football, baseball, tennis and golf. Those who see competition as a form of legalized hostility tend to favor such noncompetitive forms of recreation as surfing, frisbee or jogging. If they do play tennis or golf, they insist on doing it "noncompetitively." Their maxim is that co-operation is better than competition.

Those who argue against the value of competition have plenty of ammunition. As pointed out in the last chapter, there is a wealth of evidence showing how frenzied people tend to become in competitive situations. It is true that competition for many is merely an arena for venting aggression; it is taken as a proving ground for establishing who is the stronger, tougher or smarter. Each imagines that by beating the other he has in some way established his superiority over him, not just in a game, but as a man. What is seldom recognized is that the need to prove that you are better than someone else is based on insecurity and self-doubt. Only to the extent that one is unsure about who and what he is does he need to prove himself to himself or to others.

It is when competition is thus used as a means of creating a self-image relative to others that the worst in a person comes out; then the ordinary fears and frustrations become greatly exaggerated. If I am secretly afraid that playing badly or losing the match may be taken to mean that I am less of a man, naturally I am going to be upset with myself for missing shots. And, of course, this very uptightness will make it more difficult for me to perform at my highest levels. There would be no problem with competition if one's self-image were not at stake.

I have taught many children and teenagers who were caught up in the belief that their self-worth depended on how well they performed at tennis and other skills. For them, playing well and winning are often life-and-death issues. They are constantly measuring themselves in comparison with their friends by using their skill at tennis as one of the measuring rods. It is as if some believe that only by being the best, only by being a winner, will they be eligible for the love and respect they seek. In the process of measuring themselves and others according to their abilities, the true and measureless value of each is frequently overlooked.

Children who have been taught to measure themselves in this way often become adults driven by a compulsion to succeed which overshadows all else. The tragedy of this belief is not that they will fail to find the success they seek, but that they will not discover the love or even the self-respect they were led to believe will come with it. Furthermore, in their single-minded pursuit of measurable success, the development of many other human potentialities is sadly neglected. Some never find the time or inclination to appreciate the beauties of nature, to express their deepest feelings and thoughts to a loved one, or to wonder about the ultimate purpose of their existence.

But whereas some seem to get trapped in the compulsion to succeed, others take a rebellious stance. Pointing to the blatant cruelties and limitations involved in a cultural pattern which tends to value only the winner and ignore even the positive qualities of the mediocre, they vehemently criticize competition. Among the most vocal are youth who have suffered under competitive pressures imposed on them by parents or society. Teaching these young people, I often observe in them a desire to fail. They seem to seek failure by making no effort to win or achieve success. They go on strike, as it were. By not trying, they always have an alibi: "I may have lost, but it doesn't count because I really didn't try." What is not usually admitted is the belief that if they had really tried and lost, then yes, that *would* count. Such a loss would be a measure of their worth. Clearly this belief is the same as that of the competitor trying to prove himself. Both are ego-trips; both are based on the mistaken assumption that one's sense of self-respect rides on how well he performs in relation to others. Both are afraid of not measuring up. Only as this fundamental and often nagging fear begins to dissolve can we discover a new meaning in competition.

My own attitude toward competition went through quite an evolution before I arrived at my present point of view. As described in the last chapter I was raised to believe in competition, and both playing well and winning meant a great deal to me. But as I began applying the principles of yoga to the teaching and playing of tennis, I became noncompetitive. Instead of trying to win, I decided to attempt only to play beautifully and excellently; in other words, I began to play a rather pure form of Perfect-o. My theory was that I would be like a yogi, unconcerned with how well I was doing in relation to my opponent and absorbed solely in achieving excellence for its own sake. Very beautiful; I would waltz around the court being very fluid, accurate, and "wise."

But something was missing. I didn't experience a desire to win, and as a result I often lacked the necessary determination. I had thought that it was in the desire to win that one's ego entered the picture, but at one point I began to ask myself if there wasn't such a motivation as an ego-less desire to win. Was there a determination to win that wasn't an ego-trip and didn't involve all the fears and frustrations that accompany ego-trips? Does the will to win always have to mean "See I'm better than you"?

One day I had an interesting experience which convinced me in an unexpected way that playing for the sake of beauty and excellence was not all there was to tennis. For several weeks I had been trying to get a date with a particular girl. She had turned me down twice, but each time with what appeared to be a good reason. Finally a dinner date was set, and on that day as I finished my last lesson one of the other pros asked me to play a couple of sets. "I'd really like to, Fred," I replied, "but I can't make it this evening." At that moment I was informed there was a telephone call for me. "Hold on, Fred," I said. "If that call is what I'm afraid it is, you may have yourself a match. If so, watch out!" The call was what I'd feared. The excuse was a valid one, and the girl was so nice about it that I couldn't get angry at her, but as I hung up I realized I was furious. I grabbed my racket, ran down to the court and began hitting balls harder than I ever had before. Amazingly, most of them went in. I didn't let up when the match began, nor did I relent my all-out attack until it was over. Even on crucial points I would go for winners and make them. I was playing with an uncharacteristic determination even when ahead; in fact I was playing *out of my mind.* Somehow the anger had taken me beyond my own preconceived limitations; it took me beyond caution. After the match Fred shook my hand without looking in the least dejected. He'd run into a hurricane on that day which he couldn't handle, but he'd had fun trying. In fact, I'd played so well that he seemed glad to have been there to witness it, or as if he deserved some credit for my reaching that level—which of course he did.

But anger couldn't be the secret to ego-less tennis, or could it? I hadn't been angry at my opponent or at myself. I was simply furious in such a way that it took me out of my mind. It enabled me to play with abandon, unconcerned about winning or playing well. I just hit the damn ball, and I enjoyed the hell out of it! It was one of the most fulfilling times I'd ever had on the court. The key seemed to be that something took me beyond myself, beyond the sense of ego-trying. The kind of trying that Self 1 does to feed its self-image was gone, but in its place was a strong, unwavering determination to win. Paradoxically, winning at that point mattered less to me, but I found myself making my greatest effort.

The Meaning of Winning

The riddle of the meaning of competition didn't come clear to me until later, when I began to discover something about the nature of the will to win. The key insight into the meaning of winning occurred one day in the course of discussion with my father, who, as mentioned earlier, had introduced me to competition and had considered himself an avid competitor in the worlds of both sport and business. Many times previously we had argued about competition, with my taking the side that it was unhealthy and only brought out the worst in people. But this particular conversation transcended argument.

I began by pointing to surfing as an example of a form of recreation which didn't involve one in competitiveness. Reflecting on this remark, Dad asked, "But don't surfers in fact compete against the waves they ride? Don't they avoid the strength of the wave and exploit its weakness?"

"Yes, but they're not competing against any person; they're not trying to beat anyone," I replied.

"No, but they are trying to make it to the beach, aren't they?"

"Yes, but the real point for the surfer is to be beautiful, to get into the flow of the wave and perhaps to achieve oneness with it." But then it hit me. Dad was right; the surfer does want to ride the wave to the beach, yet he waits in the ocean for the biggest wave to come along that he thinks he can handle. If he just wanted to be beautiful, he could do that on a medium-size wave. Why does the surfer wait for the big wave? The answer was simple, and it unraveled the confusion which surrounds the true nature of competition. The surfer waits for the big wave because he values the challenge it presents. He values the obstacles the wave puts between him and his goal of riding the wave to the beach. Why? Because it is those very obstacles, the size and churning power of the wave, which draw from the surfer his greatest effort. It is only against the big waves that he is required to use all his skill, all his courage and concentration to overcome; only then can he realize the true limits of his capacities. At that point he often slips into a superconscious state and attains his peak. In other words, the more challenging the obstacle he faces, the greater the opportunity for the surfer to discover and extend his true potential. The potential may have always been within him, but until it is manifested in action, it remains a secret hidden from himself. The obstacles are a very necessary ingredient to this process of self-discovery. Note that the surfer in this example is not out to *prove* himself; he is not out to show himself or the world how great he is, but is simply involved in the exploration of his latent capacities. He directly and intimately experiences his own resources and thereby increases his self-knowledge.

From this example the basic meaning of winning became clear to me. *Winning is overcoming obstacles to reach a goal, but the value in winning is only as great as the value of the goal reached.* Reaching the goal itself may not be as valuable as the experience that can come in making a supreme effort to overcome the obstacles involved. The process can be more rewarding than the victory itself.

Once one recognizes the value of having difficult obstacles to overcome, it is a simple matter to see the true benefit that can be gained from competitive sports. In tennis who is it that provides a person with the obstacles he needs in order to experience his highest limits? His opponent, of course! Then is your opponent a friend or an enemy? He is a friend to the extent that he does his best to make things difficult for you. Only by playing the role of your enemy does he become your true friend. Only by competing with you does he in fact cooperate! No one wants to stand around on the court waiting for the big wave. In this use of competition it is the duty of your opponent to create the greatest possible difficulties for you, just as it is yours to try to create obstacles for him. Only by doing this do you give each other the opportunity to find out to what heights each can rise.

So we arrive at the startling conclusion that true competition is identical with true cooperation. Each player tries his hardest to defeat the other, but in this use of competition it isn't the other *person* we are defeating; it is simply a matter of overcoming the obstacles he presents. In true competition no person is defeated. Both players benefit by their efforts to overcome the obstacles presented by the other. Like two bulls butting their heads against one another, both grow stronger and each participates in the development of the other.

This attitude can make a lot of changes in the way you approach a tennis match. In the first place, instead of hoping your opponent is going to double-fault, you actually wish that he'll get his first serve in. This desire for the ball to land inside the line helps you to achieve a better mental state for returning it. You tend to react faster and move better, and by doing so, you make it more challenging for your opponent. You tend to build confidence in your opponent as well as in yourself and this greatly aids your sense of anticipation. Then at the end you shake hands with your opponent, and regardless of who won you thank him for the fight he put up, and you mean it.

I used to think that if I was playing a friendly match against a player with a weak backhand, it was a bit dirty to always play his weakness. In the light of the foregoing, nothing could be further from the truth! If you play his backhand as much as you can, it can only get better as a result. If you are a nice guy and play his forehand, his backhand will remain weak; in this case the real nice guy is the competitor.

This same insight into the nature of true competition led to yet another reversal in my thinking which greatly benefited my playing. Once when I was fifteen I upset an eighteen-year-old in a local tournament. After the match my father came down from the stands and heartily congratulated me for my victory, but my mother's reaction was, "Oh, that poor boy; how badly he must feel to have been beaten by someone so much younger." It was a clear example of the psyche pulled against itself. I felt pride and guilt simultaneously. Until I realized the purpose of competition, I never felt really happy about defeating someone, and mentally I had my hardest time playing well when I was near victory. I have found this to be true with many players, especially when on the verge of an upset. One cause of the uptightness experienced at these times is based on the false notion about competition. If I assume that I am making myself more worthy of respect by winning, then I must believe, consciously or unconsciously, that by defeating someone, I am making him less worthy of respect. I can't go up without pushing someone else down. This belief involves us in a needless sense of guilt. You don't have to become a killer to be a winner; you merely have to realize that killing is not the name of the game. Today I play every point to win. It's simple and it's good. I don't worry about winning or losing the match, but whether or not I am making the maximum effort during every point because I realize that that is where the true value lies.

Maximum effort does not mean the super-exertion of Self 1. It means concentration, determination and trusting your body to "let it happen." It means maximum physical and mental effort. At the point that one is going all out, he is most apt to slip "out of his mind" into the unmatchable beauty of "unconscious play." There he possesses a high awareness of the oneness of the players and the play. Again competition and cooperation become one.

The difference between being concerned about winning and being concerned about making the effort to win may seem subtle, but in the effect there is a great difference. When I'm concerned only about winning, I'm caring about something that I can't wholly control. Whether I win or lose the external game is a result of my opponent's skill and effort as well as my own. When one is emotionally attached to results that he can't control, he tends to become anxious and then try too hard. But one can control the *effort* he puts into winning. One can always do the best he can at any given moment. Since it is impossible to feel anxiety about an event that one *can* control, the mere awareness that you are using maximum effort to win each point will carry you past the problem of anxiety. As a result, the energy which would otherwise have gone into the anxiety and its consequences can then be utilized in one's effort to win the point. In this way one's chances of winning the outer game are maximized.

Thus, for the player of the Inner Game, it is the moment-by-moment effort to let go and to stay centered in the here-and-now action which offers the real winning and losing, and this game never ends. The Inner Game frees the player from concern about the fruits of victory; he becomes devoted only to the goal of self-knowledge, to the exploration of his true nature at it reveals itself on level after level.

10. The Inner Game Off the Court

Up to this point we have been exploring the Inner Game as it applies to tennis. We began with the observation that many of our difficulties in tennis are mental in origin. As tennis players we tend to think too much before and during our shots; we try too hard to control our movements; and we are too concerned about the results of our actions and how they might reflect on our self-image. In short, we worry too much and don't concentrate very well. To gain clarity on the mental problems in tennis we introduced the concept of Self 1 and Self 2. Self 1 was the name given to the conscious ego-mind which likes to tell Self 2, the body and unconscious computerlike mind, how to hit the tennis ball. The key to spontaneous, high-level tennis is in resolving the lack of harmony which usually exists between these two selves. This requires the learning of several inner skills, chiefly the art of letting go of self-judgments, letting Self 2 do the hitting, recognizing and trusting the natural learning process, and above all gaining some practical experience in the art of concentration.

At this point the concept of the Inner Game emerges. Not only can these inner skills have a remarkable effect on one's forehand, backhand, serve and volley (the outer game of tennis), but they are valuable in themselves and have broad applicability to other aspects of life. When a player comes to recognize, for instance, that learning to concentrate may be more valuable to him than a backhand, he shifts from being primarily a player of the outer game to being a player of the Inner Game. Then, instead of learning concentration to improve his tennis, he practices tennis to improve his concentration. This represents a crucial shift in values from the outer to the inner. Only when this shift occurs within a player does he free himself of the anxieties and frustrations involved in being overly dependent on the results of the external game. Only then does he have the chance to go beyond the limitations inherent in the various ego-trips of Self 1 and to reach a new awareness of his true potential. Competition then becomes an interesting device in which each player, by making his maximum effort to win, gives the other the opportunity he desires to reach new levels of self-awareness.

Thus, there are two games involved in tennis: one the outer game played against the obstacles presented by an external opponent and played for one or more external prizes; the other, the Inner Game, played against internal mental and emotional obstacles for the reward of increasing self-realization—that is, knowledge of one's true potential. It should be recognized that both the inner and outer games go on simultaneously, so the choice is not which one to play, but which deserves priority.

Clearly, almost every human activity involves both the outer and inner games. There are always external obstacles between us and our external goals, whether we are seeking wealth, education, reputation, friendship, peace on earth, or simply something to eat for dinner. And the inner obstacles are always there; the very mind we use in obtaining our external goals is easily distracted by its tendency to worry, regret or generally muddle the situation, thereby causing needless difficulties from within. It is helpful to realize that whereas our external goals are many and various and require the learning of many skills to achieve them, the inner obstacles come from only one source and the skills needed to overcome them remain constant. Self 1 is the same wherever you are and whatever you are doing. Concentration in tennis is fundamentally no different from the concentration needed to perform any task or even to enjoy a symphony; learning to let go of the habit of judging yourself on the basis of your backhand is no different from forgetting the habit of judging your child or boss; and learning to welcome obstacles in competition automatically increases one's ability to find advantage in all the difficulties one meets in the course of one's life. Hence, every inner gain applies immediately and automatically to the full range of one's activities. This is why it is worthwhile to pay some attention to the inner game.

Now it will be useful to discuss more specifically the relation of these inner skills learned in tennis to everyday life.

Unfreakability: The Art of Quieting the Mind

Perhaps the most indispensable tool for man in modern times is the ability to remain calm in the midst of rapid and unsettling changes. The person who will best survive the present age is the one Kipling described as one who can keep his head while all about are losing theirs. "Unfreakability" refers not to man's propensity for burying his head in the sand at the sight of danger, but to the ability to see the true nature of what is happening around him and to be able to respond appropriately. This requires a mind which is clear because it is calm.

"Freaking out" is a general term used for an upset mind. For example, it describes what happens in the minds of many tennis players just after they have hit a shallow lob, or while preparing to serve on match point with the memory of past double faults rushing through their minds. Freaking out is what some stock-brokers do when the market begins to plunge; what some parents do when their child has not returned from a date on time; or what most of the human population would do if they heard that beings from outer space had landed on Earth. The mind gets so upset that it does not see clearly enough what is happening to take the appropriate action. When action is born in worry and self-doubt, it is usually inappropriate and often too late to be effective.

The causes of "freak-outs" can be grouped into three categories: regret about past events; fear or uncertainty about the future; and dislike of a present event or situation. In all cases, the event and the mind's reaction to it are two separate things. It takes both to produce the result, but the freak-out is in and of the mind; it is not an attribute of the event itself.

Let's take a closer look at each of these three kinds of freak-outs. First, regret about the past. This is the "crying over spilled milk" syndrome. In this case the mind not only neglects present action, but—as demonstrated in earlier chapters—usually becomes involved in harsh self-criticism. The regret at hitting the ball into the net starts with a judgment of the event, such as "What a bad serve," but then, through a subtle, lightning-quick process of identification with the event, becomes the self-critical "I'm a bad server." In another instant a belief emerges in the player that he is uncoordinated and incompetent. Finally, since coordination is often taken as a sign of one's manhood, the player may even arrive at the conclusion that he is not very masculine. Probably the least damaging result of this chain of thought is that the player has perfectly programmed himself to hit another ball into the net at the first opportunity.

131

In freak-outs about the past we typically worry about what we can do little about at the time, then scold ourselves needlessly and end up worrying about someone else's worrying. This kind of mental process is almost universal, and if it is allowed to go its way unchecked it causes unnecessary anxiety and wastes valuable energy. It also prevents us from seeing things as they are.

Now let us look at anxiety, or the feeling of uncertainty about the future. This is the primary cause of tension and nerves on the tennis court. At a crucial point in a match, my mind, controlled by apprehension, starts thinking, If I lose this point, the score will be 5–3, and if I don't break his serve, I'll lose the set. Then I'll have a really hard time winning the match . . . I wonder how it will sound when I tell Barbara that I lost to George in straight sets . . . I can just hear the guys at the office talking about it . . . I wonder what the boss is going to think about the report I submitted . . . I really should have put more work into it . . . My position in the company isn't really that secure; I'd better buckle down next week . . . I wonder if there's any other kind of work I could do if I happened to lose this job. . . . Needless to say, such a train of thought isn't going to help me swing smoothly and naturally on my next shot; Self 1 has too much riding on it to just let it happen.

When such a mental process starts, try to stop it as soon as you recognize what is happening. The mind must be brought back to the here and now. If you have nothing better to focus your attention on, I have found it effective to concentrate my mind on the process of breathing, which automatically keeps me in the present. Another way to deal with the uncontrolled mind is to simply observe it. Attempt to stay uninvolved with your mind's trip and just see where it goes. This can be a good way to learn something about the games that Self 1 plays.

A good off-the-court example of future freak-out is what happened in my own mind as I set out to rewrite the first draft of this chapter. My editor at Random House had called me long distance to tell me that in order to meet our publishing schedule, the completed manuscript must be finished in four days. Although this gave me a few more days that I'd expected, it was still a deadline, and when the new text didn't seem to flow, I began a mild freak-out. The closer the deadline approached, the more pressure I would feel. The more pressure, the less flow; the less flow, the more pressure. I became unhappy about the results coming out of my typewriter and felt I had to read them to someone else for confirmation. When my usually doting mother fell asleep during one of these test marketings, I knew I had to start all over again. But how was I going to meet the deadline now, with less time and just as much work to do? You can imagine some of the trips my mind started to take, all stemming from worry over an imagined future event—or, more exactly, imagining that a certain future event would *not* happen. Had I not been writing on the very subject, this mental process might have seemed so normal that it would have passed by unnoticed. But I awoke the next morning realizing that the example I needed to explain freaking out over the future was within my own immediate experience, and that the solution to the pressure I was feeling was the solution for the chapter.

Once again, as in all cases, the answer begins with seeing that the problem is more in the mind than in the external situation. It wasn't the deadline that was causing the problem, but the way my mind was reacting to it. Admittedly, failing to meet the deadline would result in certain consequences, but the pressure was coming mostly from my imagined beliefs about the harm such consequences could actually do me or others. The proper function of the deadline (like death itself) is to encourage effort to accomplish one's purpose. But what function does worrying serve? Only to show me more about the nature of Self 1 and how it likes to work its way into controlling my mind and actions.

A good example of what happens when Self 1 is not allowed to interfere was given by John Newcombe as he came from behind to win the first match of the 1973 Davis Cup finals against Stan Smith. When asked after the match what he had been thinking about when he was behind, two sets to one, and with all the pressure of representing his country, Newcombe said that he wasn't thinking at all. He just felt adrenaline flowing through him, and with it something akin to anger and determination. "I became very concentrated, and the shots just seemed to flow out of me," he concluded.

As we learn to keep our minds in the present and decline to take fear trips into the future, we find that there is an automatic process which gives us the necessary resources to deal with the situation at hand. As the mind learns to remain calm in critical moments, it becomes able to distinguish easily between real and imagined danger. It is noteworthy that the same mind which causes us to worry about its own projected fantasies also frequently ignores real and present dangers. An entire population is capable of ignoring the signs of a potentially catastrophic war while it freaks out over events that are already past. To repeat, calmness does not mean lack of concern; it means the ability to separate the real from the unreal and thereby to take sensible action.

Perhaps this is an appropriate place to remind the reader that I am *not* suggesting "positive thinking" as the best means of overcoming freak-outs. To replace negative programming with positive programming by repeating such assertions as "I have a great backhand; I am going to win today," or "There is no misery and suffering in the world," only adds to the mental blur which prevents us from seeing things as they are. Positive thinking is the same kind of mental activity as negative thinking; it is the other side of the same coin and thus inextricably linked to it. If you view some events as positive, it becomes psychologically impossible not to see others as negative. The mind only adds positive and negative attributes to events when it is not satisfied to see things as they are. Such a mind distorts reality in an attempt to gain a peace which it lacks.

A gusty wind during a tennis match, a baby screaming, or a shortage of fuel are examples of the third category of freak-out—dislike of a present event. They are all annoying distractions which intrude on our consciousness at varying intervals for varying durations.

The first step Self 1 usually takes in such instances is to judge the event as unpleasant—neglecting, of course, the possibility that the "unpleasantness" may have its source in the mind rather than in the event. Then, if the event recurs or the situation continues, the mind experiences it as still more unpleasant. Next, we may try to do something to change the situation, whether it is a bad backhand or a displeasing sound, and when this does not work we approach the height of our exasperation. A loud record player in the apartment below seems annoying when it begins; it seems more so when you decide you want to read a book; but it becomes infuriating after you have gotten up, gone downstairs and, using all your diplomacy, extracted an agreement from your neighbors to keep the music lower, only to hear the music turned up to full volume again fifteen minutes later as you're getting ready for bed. This time each measure of music carries the added disturbance of direct insult to the ego.

There are only two possible approaches to dealing with upsetting circumstances in the present. One is to change the circumstance; the other is to change the mind which is experiencing the upset. Sometimes finding the appropriate way to change the circumstances is the most sensible, but the player of the Inner Game always has another option. He can realize that there is no need to give any sight or sound the power to upset him. He can choose to see the disturbance as stemming from his mind and not from the event. Then he can find a solution. For example, in the case just mentioned the man may decide to listen to and enjoy the music, or to try to tune it out, taking this opportunity to gain some practical experience in the art of concentration which will stand him in good stead in our noisy world.

There are always going to be thoughts and events that try to pull our attention away from the here and now. Each is an opportunity to practice the all-important art of concentration. As we become able to turn annoyances and apparent obstacles to our advantage in the inner game, are we not becoming freer?

The cause of all the freak-outs discussed above can be summed up in the word *attachment*. Self 1 gets so dependent on things, situations, people and concepts within his experience that when change occurs or seems about to occur, he freaks out. Freedom from mental freak-outs happens as one's peace of mind becomes more and more a function of inner resources and less and less dependent upon externals. Letting go of attachments does not mean losing anything (a child does not risk losing his thumb when he stops sucking it); it does mean releasing our grip on things and our desire to control them. Example: it is the grip on wealth which makes a miser uptight and unhappy, not the wealth itself.

Letting It Happen

A Zen master once asked an audience of Westerners what they thought was the most important word in the English language. After giving his listeners a chance to think about such favorite words as love, truth, faith, and so on, he said, "No, it's a three-letter word; it's the word 'let.' " Let it be. Let it happen. Though sometimes employed to mean a kind of passiveness, these phrases actually refer to a deep acceptance of the fundamental process inherent in life. In tennis it means trusting in the incredibly complex and competent computerlike mechanism of the human body. In the more general sense it means faith in the fundamental order and goodness of life, both human and natural.

Letting go means allowing joy to come into your life instead of contriving to have a good time; learning to appreciate the love and beauty already happening around you rather than trying to manufacture something which you think isn't there; letting problems be solved in the unconscious mind as well as by straining with conscious effort.

But perhaps where letting go is most important is in the area of human growth. Many people who read this book may be involved in one or more attempts at what may be called self-improvement.

It would be natural if they thought, Here is a book that may help my tennis, and perhaps some other areas of my life which need working on. Admittedly, much of this book may seem to read that way, but speaking as a man who once was a compulsive self-improver, I want to make it clear that the last thing I wish to do is to encourage any notion that you should be any different from what you are right now. I say this with great conviction because I spent many not-so-happy years trying to become "better" than I thought I was, trying to change into somebody I thought I should be. In my eagerness to achieve that "should" I found it easy to lose touch with the sense of who and what I truly was—and of course still am.

Many people carry around with them an image of the kind of person they wish they were, much as a tennis player imagines the kind of serve he wishes he could deliver. When our behavior does not seem to measure up to our ideal, we grow dejected and then start trying hard to correct it ("Perhaps I should take a series of lessons, or a course on personality development, or read a book about how to become less self-critical, or undergo therapy, or join an encounter group"). Such steps are not necessarily foolish—I have taken them all—but what is needed is not so much the effort to improve ourselves, as the effort to become more aware of the beauty of what we already are. As we begin to see and appreciate our essential selves, we manifest automatically that beauty and our true capacities, simply by letting them happen.

This approach may sound too simplistic to be practical, and I don't wish to give the impression that discovering one's essential self can be done simply by agreeing with concepts written in a book. But I see tennis players every day trying hard to correct their "faulty" games, and they learn at a much slower rate than the player who places his confidence in whatever potential is already within him and then lets it happen. Both have to practice, but the first type is beset with problems of self-doubt trying to make himself into something he's afraid he isn't, bearing all the credit and blame for the results. In contrast, I see the second player trusting the potential within himself and learning to rely on the natural process by which that potential becomes actual. He trusts Self 2 to learn to play the game, and as a result gains a very practical confidence in this process within him which he didn't consciously produce. In this way he becomes confident, yet remains humble. Any and all credit goes to Self 2, not Self 1.

In respect to my own growth, whether in tennis or any other aspect of development, I have found it helpful to look at myself as the seed of a tree, with my entire potential already within me, as opposed to a building, which must have stories added to it to achieve a greater height. This makes it easier for me to see that it doesn't help me to try to be what I'm not at any given moment, or to form concepts of what I *should* be, or to compare myself to the other trees around me. I can understand that I need only use all the rain and sunshine that come my way, and cooperate fully with the seed's impulse to develop and manifest what it already uniquely is.

Letting go in this sense means letting go of our attachment to the idea of controlling our own development; the only other example I will give here could be called letting go of the final attachment.

One cold winter evening, I drove from New Hampshire to a small town in northern Maine. On my way back at about midnight, I skidded on an icy curve and spun my Volkswagen gently but firmly off the road into a snowbank.

As I sat in the car getting colder by the second, the gravity of my situation struck me. It was about twenty degrees below zero outside, and I had nothing other than the sports jacket I was wearing. There was no hope of keeping warm in the car while it was stationary, and there was little hope of being picked up by another car. It had been twenty minutes since I had passed through a town, and not a single automobile had passed me in that time. There were no farmhouses, no cultivated land, not even telephone poles to remind me of civilization. I had no map and no idea how far ahead the next town might be.

I was faced with an interesting existential choice. I would freeze if I remained in the car, so I had to decide whether to walk forward into the unknown in the hope that a town might be around the very next corner, or to walk back in the direction from which I had come, knowing that there was certain help at least fifteen miles back. After deliberating for a moment, I decided to take my chances with the unknown. After all, isn't that what they do in the movies? I walked forward for about ten steps and then, without thinking, pivoted decisively and walked back the other way.

After three minutes, my ears were freezing and felt as if they were about to chip off, so I started to run. But the cold drained my energy quickly, and soon I had to slow again to a walk. This time I walked for only two minutes before becoming too cold. Again I ran, but again grew fatigued quickly. The periods of running began to grow shorter, as did the periods of walking, and I soon realized what the outcome of these decreasing cycles would be. I could see myself by the side of the road covered with snow, frozen to death. At that moment, what had first appeared to be merely a difficult situation began to look as if it was going to be my *final* situation. Awareness of the very real possibility of death slowed me to a stop.

After a minute of reflection I found myself saying aloud, "Okay, if now is the time, so be it. I'm ready." I really meant it. With that I stopped thinking about it and began walking calmly down the road, suddenly aware of the beauty of the night. I became absorbed in the silence of the stars and in the loveliness of the dimly lit forms around me; everything was beautiful. Then without thinking, I started running. To my surprise I didn't stop for a full forty minutes, and then only because I spotted a light burning in the window of a distant house.

Where had this energy come from which allowed me to run so far without stopping? I hadn't felt frightened; I simply didn't get tired. As I relate this story now, it seems that saying "I accepted death" is ambiguous. I didn't give up in the sense of quitting. In one sense I gave up caring; in another I seemed to care more. Apparently, letting go of my grip on life released an energy which paradoxically made it possible for me to run with utter abandon *toward* life.

"Abandon" is a good word to describe what happens to a tennis player who feels he has nothing to lose. He stops caring about the outcome and plays all out. This is the true meaning of detachment. It means letting go of the concern of Self 1 and letting the natural concern of a deeper self take over. It is caring, yet not caring; it is effortless effort. It happens when one lets go of attachment to the results of one's actions and allows the increased energy to come to bear on the action itself. In the language of karma yoga, this is called action without attachment to the fruits of action, and ironically when the state is achieved the results are the best possible.

Concentration and Higher Consciousness

A woman walks into a dark room and sees a snake coiled ominously in the middle of the floor. She panics and calls for her son. When the son comes he turns on the light in the room and the woman sees only a coiled rope.

In the foregoing sections on unfreakability and letting it happen, the essential art to be learned was shown to be that of becoming increasingly aware of things *as they are.* The ghosts of the past and the monsters of the future disappear when all one's conscious energy is employed in understanding the present. The light which dispels the shadows of our mental projections is the light of our own consciousness. When we understand something, we may have cause to be wary of it, but there is no fear. Understanding the present moment, the only time when any action can occur, requires concentration of mind: the ability to keep the mind focused in the here and now.

In Chapter 7 I spoke of consciousness as the energy of light which makes an experience knowable, just as a light bulb in the forest illuminates its surroundings. The brighter the light, the more that is known or understood about one's experience. When the light is dim because some of our energy is leaking into regrets over the past or fears of the future, or is in some way wasted in resisting the flow of life, then one's experience is filled with shadows and distortions. But when most of our conscious energy is brought to bear on the present with a sincere desire to understand what is before us, then something called "higher consciousness" occurs. It is called "higher" merely because more is seen and understood than before. It is something like walking up a mountain and having an increasing view of what is going on in the valley below — except that in the case of increased consciousness you are not only able to see more because of your point of view, but you can also see the subtler details with greater clarity. Thus the art of concentration is basically the art of experiencing ever more fully whatever is in the here and now for you.

Concentration is said to be the master art because all other arts depend on it; progress in this, as in any art, is achieved only through practice. I have found tennis an enjoyable arena for practicing concentration, but there is in fact no life situation where one cannot practice focusing one's full attention on what is happening at the moment. Normally, we tend to concentrate only when something we consider important is happening, but the player of the Inner Game recognizes increasingly that *all* moments are important ones and worth paying attention to, for each moment can increase his understanding of himself and life.

What makes it possible to learn more from ordinary experience? Two people witness the same sunset; one has a deep experience of beauty, and the other, perhaps because his mind is preoccupied, has a minimal experience. Two people read the same lines in a book; one recognizes a profound truth while the other finds nothing worth remembering. One day we get out of bed and the world looks full of beauty and interest; the next day everything appears drab. In each case the difference lies in our own state of consciousness. In the final analysis it is our state of consciousness which is the determining factor in our appreciation of the beautiful, the true, or the loving. A man may own an exquisite oil painting, but if he can't appreciate its beauty, how valuable really is that painting to him? Another man may own nothing beautiful, but if his consciousness is attuned to beauty, he is rich because he will always be surrounded by beauty.

I was once asked: "In a conversation between a fool and a wise man, who learns the most?" Being a teacher at the time, I was quick to think that since the wise man had more to offer, the fool would benefit the most, but then I saw that the opposite was in fact true. The fool is a fool because he doesn't know how to learn from his experience; the wise man is wise because he does. Therefore the wise man will learn more from the conversation than the fool. Then it became clear to me that if I wasn't learning as much as my tennis students in the course of a lesson, I probably shouldn't be teaching them. This notion gave me an entirely new perspective on teaching. I began paying attention not only to backhands and forehands, but to the process of learning itself. It was only because my students taught me something about the learning process that this book could be written.

Each of the above examples points to the value of the Inner Game. Every heightening of consciousness enables one to appreciate more fully the experiences which life offers each player. Changes in consciousness alter our lives automatically because it is only through consciousness that we experience life.

The Goal of the Inner Game: The Discovery of Self 3

Now we come to an interesting point—and the last one: out of all the human experiences possible, which does the player of the inner game pursue? Even in the here and now there are almost limitless choices about what to focus one's attention upon. What do we really want to tune in to? What do we really want to see and hear, and what do we really want to do? These are the questions that the player of the inner game finally arrives at and continues to ask himself until he has found his answer. Found what? *That which he can love and that which gives complete satisfaction.* For only when man is paying attention to something he really loves can he concentrate his mind and find true satisfaction.

So the search is on, the search for the goal of the inner game. Players of the game have given many names to this goal. Some call it self-knowledge, some call it soul, others reality. It has been called Peace, Truth, Love, Joy, Beauty, Super-Consciousness, and God, as well as many other names in other cultures. But the name is not important because no one has ever found satisfaction by repeating the name; nor have labels helped people learn where to look or how to find that which the names refer to. Those who have experienced the reality behind the label say that it is beyond names which can be spoken and beyond a beauty which can be described. It has been found by the learned and the untutored, the rich and the poor, the Easterner and the Westerner. Apparently the only qualifications for this discovery have been that the seeker be human and have the will and good fortune to find the way.

When one undertakes the quest for this priceless treasure, when one searches for the secret which is capable of meeting the deepest longing within his heart, then he has truly embarked on the Inner Game. At that point, all the inner skills described in this book will be of help, but the player's most valuable assets will be his sincerity and determination.

My own experience is that the true goal of the Inner Game is to be found within. Nothing outside of ourselves is ever permanent enough or sufficient to satisfy completely, but there is something within every human being that is not mentioned in psychology books. It is not a concept, a belief, or something that can be written in words. It is something real and changeless; its beauty and its value have no limits. It is the very source of all our potential; it is the seed from which our lives grow. It is the origin of every experience we have ever had of love, truth or beauty. Its presence within can be intuited, deduced and read about, and it can be experienced directly. When one finds one's way to the direct experience of it, when one can actually meet face to face with the essence of his life, then he has achieved the first—but not the final—goal of the Inner Game.

When the lighthouse of the home port is in sight, the ship's radar can be turned off and navigation aids set aside. What remains is to keep the lighthouse in sight and simply sail toward it. The biggest surprise in my search for the inner self was finding that it could be experienced by any human being whenever his desire for it was sufficiently sincere. This sincere desire alone will lead one to the discovery of a practical method for uncovering what could be called Self 3. Then the only instrument required is the human body itself in which consciousness is able to be aware of itself. The search is within, and the lighthouse can be seen no matter how near or far from home port one actually appears to be in terms of his own physical, emotional or spiritual development. Realizing this goal is within the capabilities of all of us and not the special privilege of any elite.

When the player of the Inner Game has searched for and found his way to the direct experience of Self 3, he gains access to the catalyst capable of finally stilling his mind. Then his full potential as a human being is allowed to unfold without interference from Self 1. He plays the rest of the game in the increasing joy of expressing with love his unique humanness, and in accordance with his own given talents and circumstances.

He is free.

About the Author

W. Timothy Gallwey was born in 1938 in San Francisco. After fifteen years of "exhausting overachievement," he missed one more easy volley—this time on match point in the National Junior Championships at Kalamazoo, Michigan. He wondered why, and the question took on symbolic importance for him. A quixotic search for truth, beauty and A's at Harvard, where he was captain of the tennis team, left this question unanswered. Then, ten years later, after leaving a career in college administration and continuing his quest throughout Europe and Asia, Mr. Gallwey finally gave up his search for an answer—and only then did his answer find him. His discovery led to the development of "yoga tennis" at the John Gardiner Tennis Ranch and the Esalen Sports Center in California, to the founding of the Inner Game Institute, and to the writing of this book.